CHELTENHAM
TOWN
365

JON PALMER

First published 2013

The History Press
The Mill, Brimscombe Port
Stroud, Gloucestershire, GL5 2QG
www.thehistorypress.co.uk

British Library Cataloguing in Publication Data.

A catalogue record for this book is available from the British Library.

ISBN 978 0 7524 6334 6

Typesetting and origination by The History Press

ACKNOWLEDGEMENTS

Thanks to Carol and Keith Palmer; Colette, Camille, Candice and Carissa; Lauren, Howie, Xanthe, Noah, Paige and Caius; Murry Toms; Laura Fell; Donna and Naomi Grabham; Hazel Lewis; Luke Court; Shaun and Sue McManus; Gareth Price; Paul Watson; Dawn and Leslie Stanley; Alan Franklin; Rachel Grisedale; Matt Holdback; Scott Rogers; Jo Tweed; Sam Smart; Mark Yates; Phil Norris; the *Gloucestershire Echo*; Sonia Yarnton; and the staff at Caffé Nero, Cheltenham.

FOREWORD

I don't have a particularly good memory – I can barely
remember what happened yesterday – but this book,
looking back on 365 days of Cheltenham Town, brought back
fond memories of both my playing and managerial career at
the club. It has also made me focus on the here and now;
creating success today which will create fond memories for
future generations.

I don't think I played particularly well when I first came
to the club. I wasn't as influential as I would like to have
been, but it was good to feel wanted. Steve Cotterill paid
a fee for me to transfer from Kidderminster. He wanted
leaders and a team who knew what they were doing.
He was trying to add the final touches to make sure we got
promoted to League Football.

Promotion to the Football League was a bittersweet
moment for me. I played for Cheltenham for four months
before we were promoted and I already knew that I was
part of a very good squad. But I didn't have my finest four
months. I struggled with injury, which was a reaction to a
firmer pitch at Whaddon Road, and I had a bit of an Achilles

heel problem. Although I didn't feature in the game against Yeovil Town when we clinched promotion (I was an unused substitute), I can remember winning and feeling proud to be a part of it.

It was an honour to be a part of Cheltenham's first League game against Rochdale in August 1999 and there was big excitement before the game. However, it is never good to lose. Rochdale were a decent side, but we didn't really play as well as we could have done and it ended in a 2–0 defeat. I think the occasion hindered the team. We knew we needed to play better if we were to stay in the League.

The 2002 play-off final against Rushden & Diamonds FC was special, especially as I was named captain. Chris Banks had been our skipper but had to miss quite a bit of the end part of the season through injury, so it was a great honour to lead out the team at the Millennium Stadium. To be on the winning team in the play-off final was brilliant. Martin Devaney scored and ripped his top off. John Finnigan smashed one in and Julian Alsop got the other. It was very, very special.

Becoming caretaker manager as Graham Allner left was a funny one for me. Graham was a really good mentor, but for whatever reason, it didn't quite work for him here. That season, he took over a team that had been promoted and it was really tough.

The day before I was asked to be caretaker manager, Lee Williams, Neil Howarth and I didn't leave a curry house until 2 a.m. Lee, or possibly Neil, was bare chested because they'd had a curry thrown over them. We'd had quite a few beers and came in the next day a little worse for wear, knowing it was time to get working and run it off. You could do that then! I then got told by the chairman that Graham had been relieved of his duties and wanted me to take charge. I probably wasn't the best person for that at that moment!

It wasn't something I particularly wanted to do that at that stage in my career, but someone had to take charge. I asked Chris Banks and Bob Bloomer to help me out, and we did it together. It was a little taster for me.

I left Cheltenham when John Ward took on the manager's role. Being on this side of it now, I fully understand why managers make those decisions. I probably thought I should have been involved at the time, but I wasn't getting a game. It was just right that I moved on. This club had been very kind to me and I think I'd done my part for the club as well. We parted on good company and I went back to Kidderminster and finished my playing career there.

I was delighted to be offered the job as manager for Cheltenham in December 2009. I was ready for a fresh start and Cheltenham is a club very close to my heart. Managing the side has created more memories.

Matches like Tottenham away in the FA Cup, the play-off final at Wembley last season and Everton at home – also in the FA Cup – obviously stand out.

Tottenham was fantastic. To take a team to play at a Premier League ground is a fantastic experience and we didn't disgrace ourselves. The team gave a good account of themselves against a quality opposition.

We were a little bit disappointed not to go up automatically at the end of the 2011/12 season.

We just couldn't quite get over the line and our poor March run cost us.

However to respond in the way we did – to beat Torquay and to take the club to Wembley – was fantastic, and the support was fantastic too. We made the club some money and the players had a great experience.

We could have won at Wembley. We had plenty of chances to win, but on the day our luck was out. We hit the crossbar, we had shots cleared off the line by bodies and by the keeper. It could so easily have been different. However, I would have been even more disappointed had we gone there and not shown what we were about. The good thing for me was that we played exceptionally well.

A promising thing to take from that, however, is that we have responded really positively and we had no hangover. We tried to improve the squad again and I think we did that last season.

The characters at the club, the people we've met and the friends we've made; they are the great memories that stick out in my mind. We've got a lot of the old players still around the place, like Russ Milton, Jamie Victory, Steve Book and Neil Howarth, and we still speak to Chris Banks, who is now on the physiotherapy staff at Stoke City.

You get constant reminders of the good times that we had, and we do talk about promotions and successful times at the club. They create a bond and a spirit amongst the team and you can say you really trusted that group of players. That's what we're trying to get here at the moment. We try to improve every year with what we've got, and I hope our supporters have enjoyed it.

There's a real family spirit about the place, a real camaraderie. We enjoy each other's company and enjoy working hard together. That's the most important thing.

Cheltenham Town is a great football club where values do mean something. We laugh every day. I'm not a great storyteller, but there have been some brilliant people at the club and some fantastic memories.

It is a privilege to write the foreword for Jon's book. Like any good journalist, Jon likes to be first with a story, but I get on very well with him. I am coy and I'm guarded, but I trust Jon with everything. He has been covering the club for a long time now and he's well respected by all the players. I listen to his interviews, he asks inquisitive questions, and above all, it is good to have a familiar face who we can trust and divulge information to. Jon is one of the good guys and more than qualified, given his passion and experience, to write about the history of a club like Cheltenham Town.

Mark Yates, Cheltenham Town Manager

JANUARY

1 January 1994

Cheltenham Town beat arch rivals Gloucester City 3–1 at Meadow Park with 2 goals from Jimmy Smith and one from Simon Cooper. The win put them top of a table for the first time in more than eight years. Tony Cook replied for the Tigers and 1,239 patrons were there to watch it. Cheltenham were in the frame for the title for most of the season, but lost out to Farnborough Town, finishing as runners-up for the second year in succession after their relegation from the Conference.

1 January 1998

A club Conference record 17-match unbeaten streak ended at Yeovil Town, where Cheltenham Town were beaten 3–1. Their previous best undefeated streak at that level was 8. The match at Huish Park is best remembered for the strong wind which caused a goal kick from Steve Book to blow back off the pitch for a corner. Cheltenham had beaten Yeovil 2–0 at home five days earlier, thanks to Clive Walker's brace.

2 January 1937

Cheltenham crashed to a 10–2 defeat at the hands of Stourbridge in the Worcestershire Senior Cup. Parry and Willmore found the net for the Robins, who went on to finish 11th in the Southern League that season.

3 January 1976

One of the smallest crowds ever to see a Cheltenham Town first team game were present as they won 2–1 at Bedworth United in the Southern League Division One (North). Only eighty-four paying customers watched Dave Lewis and Keiron Hehir score the goals to earn Cheltenham a win over the Greenbacks.

3 January 1983

Cheltenham registered their 11th successive win (8th in the league), seeing off Southern League Midland Division newcomers Dudley Town 3–0 on their way to the title. They did however lose their next match 4–0 to Merthyr Tydfil.

3 January 2000

The Robins' first match of the new millennium ended in disappointment as Lincoln City overcame a squad weakened by illness 2–0 at Whaddon Road. The Imps' goals came from Paul Miller in the 31st minute and John Finnigan in the 73rd. Finnigan went on to captain Cheltenham after making the switch from Sincil Bank to Whaddon Road in March 2002.

3 January 2001

Fulham brought a reserve team including six full internationals to Cheltenham and won 5–0, with Karl-Heinz Riedle, Kit Symons, Marcus Hahnemann and Terry Phelan among the star-studded line-up. Shane Duff was among the young Robins' second string to benefit from such an experience.

4 January 1992

Paul Evans, a Welsh striker who only played 3 games for Cheltenham after joining from Barry Town, scored his only goal for the club in a 1–1 draw with Yeovil Town. Cheltenham: Livingstone, Masefield, Willetts, N. Smith, Vircavs, Howells, Brooks, Bloomfield, Evans, Casey, Purdie.

4 January 2003

Graham Allner took charge of his 32nd and last game as Cheltenham Town manager, a 4–0 FA Cup third-round hammering at Sheffield United. On target for the Blades were Shaun Murphy, Jon-Paul McGovern and Steve Kabba (2).

4 January 2004

Cheltenham took an early lead against Fulham through Grant McCann's stunning 5th-minute strike at Loftus Road. But the Premier League club hit back with a brace from Louis Saha to progress to the fourth round of the FA Cup. His winner arrived in the final minute, breaking Cheltenham hearts. Left-back Jamie Victory did a sterling job of containing Fulham's in-form winger Steed Malbranque, while Damian Spencer gave a tireless performance up front on his own, never giving the Cottagers' back four a moment's peace.

5 January 1980

Dave Lewis was on target, but it was not enough to stop Cheltenham slipping to a 2–1 defeat at Bridgend Town in the Southern League Midland Division in front of 150 fans.

5 January 1985

Mark Boyland fired a hat-trick in a 6–0 home drubbing of AP Leamington in front of 479 spectators. Brian Hughes, Ray Baverstock and Andy Lightstone were also on the scoresheet.

6 January 1996

Second-half goals from Darren Wright and Jason Eaton earned Cheltenham a 2–1 Dr Marten's League Premier Division win over Chelmsford City at Whaddon Road. Cheltenham: Davis, Bloomer, Benton, Banks, Dunphy, Wright, Wring, Cooper, Eaton, Smith, Howell.

6 January 2002

Two goals from the mercurial Tony Naylor earned Cheltenham a shock 2–1 FA Cup third-round victory over Oldham Athletic at Whaddon Road. It took them into the fourth round for the first time in the club's history. Steve Cotterill's side went into the match undefeated in 6 matches and beaten only three times in 23 games in all competitions. Naylor opened the scoring in the 25th minute, having passed a fitness test on the morning of the game. His strike partner-in-crime, Julian Alsop, flicked on a goal kick from Steve Book and Naylor rounded defender Scott McNiven before slotting the ball in at the near post from 15 yards. Oldham equalised two minutes before half-time through David Eyres, but Cheltenham were the better side and they were rewarded for almost constant pressure when Naylor hit the winner after an hour. He was at the far post when a curling cross from Lee Williams floated over and his header went inside the post off the body of central defender Stuart Balmer. Cheltenham: Book, Griffin, M. Duff, Banks, Victory, Williams, Yates, Howells, Milton, Naylor (Grayson), Alsop. Subs not used: Brough, Higgs, Devaney, Howarth.

7 January 1984

Two second-half goals in the space of three minutes earned Cheltenham a 2–1 win over Dorchester Town in the Southern League Premier Division. Ray Baverstock scored from the spot and the second was added by Nick Gazzard, a player signed from what was then St Paul's College of Higher Education.

7 January 1995

Christer Warren's fine solo effort helped Lindsay Parsons' Cheltenham earn a 2–0 home success against Gravesend & Northfleet. Martin Boyle netted the other goal in front of a crowd of 827.

7 January 2006

Goalkeeper Scott Brown made his first appearance for Cheltenham Town in a 2–2 FA Cup third-round tie against Chester City, replacing the injured Shane Higgs. J.J. Melligan and John Finnigan were Cheltenham's scorers – both from the penalty spot.

7 January 2013

Cheltenham welcomed Premier League Everton to the Abbey Business Stadium for a televised FA Cup third-round tie. A sell-out crowd of 6,891, including 1,101 visitors, saw David Moyes' team prevail 5–1, providing the Robins with a lesson in clinical finishing. They opened up a two-goal lead in the first half through Nikica Jelavic's poacher's finish and Leighton Baines' penalty after Alan Bennett was adjudged to have fouled Marouane Fellaini. Leon Osman made it 3–0 before Russ Penn pulled one back for Cheltenham, but strikes from Seamus Coleman and Fellaini completed the comprehensive win. It was skipper Bennett's final appearance for Cheltenham before leaving the club by mutual consent on the final day of the January transfer window.

8 January 1977

Dave Lewis, Keiron Hehir and Terry Paterson scored in a 3–0 home win over Stourbridge in the Southern League Division One. The result helped the Robins towards promotion to the Premier Division that season as runners-up to Worcester City. Cheltenham: Miles, Murphy, Dangerfield, Foster, Dean, Gardner, Paterson, Lewis, Hehir, Davies, Thomas.

8 January 1986

Cheltenham signed John Powell from Kidderminster Harriers for £3,000.

8 January 1994

Neil Smith made his 100th appearance for Cheltenham Town in a 1–1 draw against Hastings. He had joined the Robins from Lincoln City in 1991.

8 January 2000

Steve Book made his 150th appearance for the club in a 2–1 victory at Macclesfield Town.

9 January 1995

Jimmy Smith, Jimmy Wring and Chris Banks all scored in a 3–3 Dr Marten's Cup third-round draw with Gresley Rovers. Cheltenham drew the second leg 2–2, bowing out on away goals, despite the tie originally being only one leg!

9 January 1997

Chris Robinson swooped to sign striker John Symonds from Bedworth.

9 January 1999

Cheltenham's run of 7 Conference games without conceding was ended at Doncaster Rovers' Belle Vue ground, where John Brough was sent off in a 2–2 draw. Dale Watkins scored both of the Robins' goals.

10 January 1999

Cheltenham's squad flew to Marbella for a mid-season break in the sun, aiding their ultimately successful Conference title push under boss Steve Cotterill.

10 January 2008

A £150,000 move to Crewe Alexandra for Damian Spencer fell through after the forward failed a medical with the Railwaymen.

11 January 1974

Dave Lewis helped himself to a hat-trick in a 7–1 FA Trophy first-round win over Bromsgrove Rovers. He was on target in the next round too, but Cheltenham went down 4–1 to Romford. Further goals came from Ken Skeen, Dave Dangerfield, Joe McDonnell and Pat Casey in front of a crowd of 1,143.

11 January 1997

Former Bedworth striker John Symonds found the net on his debut in a 3–2 home win over Baldock Town. Mark Freeman was also on target, along with a Colin Omogbehin own goal. Cheltenham: Gannaway, Wotton, Wring, Banks, Freeman, Victory, Chenoweth, Wright, Boyle, Symonds, Bloomer.

11 January 2008

Alex Russell and Steve Brooker both joined Cheltenham on loan from Bristol City and the pair played a key role in helping the club avoid relegation from League One for a second successive season.

12 January 2008

David Bird's dramatic late winner sank relegation rivals Bournemouth and earned Cheltenham 3 precious points in their battle against the drop.

13 January 1934

The largest crowd ever to watch Cheltenham for a home fixture gathered for the visit of Blackpool in the FA Cup third round. Blackpool had been relegated from the top flight the previous season, and the unprecedented interest in the match meant it was switched to the Cheltenham Athletic Ground. No sporting event in Cheltenham's history had so captured the imagination of the public as the FA Cup run of that season. Special road and rail facilities were provided to cope with the influx of football enthusiasts from far and wide. More than 10,000 fans descended on Cheltenham's temporary home to witness history in the making. Cheltenham put up a great fight, but Blackpool ran out 3–1 winners. Payne's goal gave the home side the lead within five minutes of kick-off, raising hopes of an upset. However, the superior class of the Seasiders was clearly evident in the second half and goals from Bussey, Watson and Doherty took them through to the fourth round. The crowd was 10,389. Cheltenham: Davis, Jones, Williams, Long, Blackburn, Goodger, Payne, Knight, Yarwood, Evans, Hill.

13 January 1974

Dave Lewis scored 5 goals in an 8–1 win over Wellingborough Town in front of 888 fans, who turned out for a Sunday fixture. The other goals came from Pat Casey, Billy Bailey and an own goal.

13 January 1990

On-loan winger Steve Mardenborough scored twice and Andy Gray once as Gravesend & Northfleet were beaten 5–1 at home in the FA Trophy first round. Mark Buckland and an own goal accounted for the rest of the scoreline as Conference side Cheltenham disposed of the Southern Leaguers en route to a third-round defeat against Kingstonian.

13 January 1998

A gate of exactly 6,000 turned out at Whaddon Road, the highest since 1957, to see Steve Cotterill's team hold Reading to a 1–1 draw in the FA Cup third round. Dale Watkins' penalty put Cheltenham in front before Trevor Morley took the tie to a replay, which the Royals won 2–1. Cheltenham: Book, Duff, Victory, Banks, Freeman, Knight, Howells, Walker (Eaton), Smith (Benton), Watkins, Bloomer. Subs not used: Crisp, Wright, Milton.

14 January 1967

Cheltenham lost 5–1 to Nuneaton Borough, their heaviest home defeat since April 1954.

14 January 1981

Charlie Green scored twice and Malcolm Kavanagh netted the other as Cheltenham beat Enderby Town 3–2 at Whaddon Road in the Southern League Midland Division. Green was popular during his brief spell at Cheltenham and is now chief executive at Rangers. Cheltenham: Latchford, Buckland, Dyer, Ollis, Hams, Kavanagh, MacKenzie, Tester, Green, Pemberton, Hardcastle.

14 January 1989

Peter Shearer's goal earned Cheltenham a 1–0 win at Fisher Athletic's Surrey Docks Stadium in the first round of the FA Trophy. Cheltenham: Mogg, Willetts, Burns, Craig, Vircavs, Whelan, Crowley, Eves, Walsh, Buckland, Jordan.

15 January 1947

Peter Goring's brace helped Cheltenham see off Millwall 7–3 at home, with further goals from Parris (2), Crisp, Roberts and Crowe.

15 January 1983

Dave Lewis made his 500th Robins appearance against Pwllheli and District, scoring twice in a 6–0 win. It took his record haul to 284. He ended the season with a remarkable record of 290 goals from 518 appearances. Paul Tester was top scorer in Lewis' final season, with 25.

16 January 1988

Brett Angell scored his final goals for Cheltenham Town, notching up two in a 5–3 defeat at Wycombe Wanderers. Steve Brooks scored the other.

16 January 1999

An injury-time goal from big defender Mark Freeman knocked Canvey Island out of the FA Trophy and took holders Cheltenham into the fourth round.

17 January 1948

Peter Goring made his final appearance for Cheltenham and scored in a 1–1 draw at Chelmsford before leaving to join Arsenal.

17 January 2006

Kayode Odejayi was the hero as Cheltenham won 1–0 at Chester City to secure themselves a plum FA Cup fourth-roundhome tie with Newcastle United.

17 January 2007

Match-winner in the 2006 play-off final triumph Steve Guinan was placed on the transfer list and joined Hereford United on loan a week later.

18 January 1936

Cheltenham took part in a 5–5 Southern League Cup draw with Yeovil & Petters United. R. Edwards scored four, with Black also on target.

18 January 1994

Jimmy Smith, signed from Salisbury City for £4,000, netted his 50th goal for Cheltenham in a 3–1 home win over Halesowen Town. The Scotsman went on to become the second-highest scorer in the club's history behind Dave Lewis.

18 January 1997

Chris Robinson oversaw his final match as manager, a 2–1 defeat by Dulwich Hamlet in the FA Trophy first round at Whaddon Road.

18 January 2003

Chris Banks, Mark Yates and Bob Bloomer took caretaker charge for a League One match against Cardiff City following the departure of Graham Allner. Peter Thorne gave the Bluebirds the lead after eight minutes, but John Finnigan levelled for Cheltenham in the 19th minute. Robert Earnshaw won it for the home side with a 36th minute strike at Ninian Park.

18 January 2013

Cheltenham travelled north in atrocious conditions to take on Morecambe in a Friday night fixture, battling against snow and ice. The match at the Globe Arena finished goalless.

19 January 2002

Goals from Jamie Victory and Julian Alsop earned Cheltenham a 2–0 win at Leyton Orient on their way to promotion from League Two via the play-offs for the first time.

20 January 1998

More than 2,000 travelling fans witnessed a heroic performance by the Robins, which unfortunately ended in a 2–1 FA Cup third-round replay defeat at Reading. With a fourth-round trip to Cardiff City at stake, Cheltenham gave a tremendous effort against a side three levels above them in the pyramid. Trevor Morley put Reading ahead in the 38th minute, but cup veteran Clive Walker scored an equaliser six minutes after half-time as Cheltenham dared to dream of a major upset. Walker darted in at the far post after Jason Eaton had headed back Dale Watkins' cross from the left. Martyn Booty broke Cheltenham hearts in the 72nd minute with a long-range winner. Seven minutes from the end, Jamie Victory's shot was going wide, but it hit Watkins and was diverted at speed against the inside of the near post as Cheltenham went within a whisker of taking the tie to extra-time. Almost 10,000 people stood and saluted Cotterill's braves, with the home fans applauding the non-leaguers, even chanting Chelt-en-ham in the way they had heard it from the proud travelling masses. Cotterill told his devastated players to hold their heads high after the game and assured them that they would be going to Wembley in the FA Trophy in May, which of course they did.

21 January 1978

A goal from Dave Dangerfield after sixty-one minutes was not enough to prevent Cheltenham Town falling to their 8th defeat of the season against Grantham. Cheltenham: Evans, Murphy, Edwards, Foster, Dean, Collicutt, Rice, Dangerfield, Lewis, Bryant, Hall.

21 January 1982

Reserve team boss Roger Thorndale, holder of Cheltenham's record for the most appearances, took temporary charge for a fixture against Epsom and Ewell following the sacking of Alan Grundy. Cheltenham fell 2–0 down before strikes from Normal Pemberton and Kevin Garthwaite, only for Tommy Tuite to net an injury-time winner for Epsom. Cheltenham: N. Berry, Boxall, Dyer, Castleton, Tucker, Garthwaite, MacKenzie, Pemberton, Reed, Buckland, Tester.

22 January 1979

Dave Lewis earned the nickname the 'Flying Pig' after starring in goal for Cheltenham in a famous 2–1 FA Trophy win at mighty Altrincham. Dennis Brown, a £1,000 signing from Margate, scored twice and Lewis performed heroics between the sticks, showing he could save as well as score goals. Regular number one Jeff Miles was a building society manager in the Welsh town of Aberdare and he was unable to take the time off work to travel, but boss Denis Allen only found this out at lunchtime on the day of the tie. Allen was banking on Miles' understudy Nigel Berry turning up at Moss Lane, but it soon became apparent he was not going to make it either. Lewis, who had already netted 247 goals in 405 starts in his more accustomed striking role, donned the goalkeeping jersey, along with a pair of woollen tracksuit bottoms, for the first time in his life. With none other than the legendary England World Cup winning goalkeeper Gordon Banks watching in disbelief from the stands, twenty-six-year-old Lewis gave an incredible performance to shut out one of the most formidable teams in non-league football at the time. Banks was overheard saying: 'Well, he is different, isn't he!' as Lewis volleyed shots away in almost comical fashion. Despite being remembered for his incredible goalscoring feats, when questioned, Lewis singles out this match as the one that stands out above all others as his most magical memory in a Cheltenham shirt. Who would have thought that shirt would have been green. Cheltenham: Lewis, Murphy, Bayliffe, Coslett, Dean, Foster, McKenzie, Dangerfield, Payne, Davies, Brown.

22 January 1994

A towering header from Steve Jones was enough to knock Nuneaton Borough out of the FA Trophy. Cheltenham: Thomas, Bloomer, S. Jones, Tucker, N. Smith, Brown, Howells, Owen, J. Smith, Warren, Lovell.

22 January 1997

Chris Robinson was sacked as Cheltenham Town boss and Steve Cotterill took charge as caretaker manager, heralding the start of the most progressive era in the club's history.

22 January 1998

Dale Watkins scored a hat-trick in a 5–1 FA Trophy first-round replay win over Enfield. Keith Knight and Clive Walker were the other scorers. Cheltenham: Book, Duff, Victory, Banks, Freeman, Knight, Howells, Smith, Eaton, Watkins, Bloomer.

22 January 1999

Cheltenham suffered the first home defeat of their Conference title-winning campaign, going down 1–0 to Northwich Victoria.

22 January 2000

Martin Devaney scored his first goal for Cheltenham to rescue a point at Hull City, who had taken the lead after thirty-five seconds through Jamaican international Theodore Whitmore.

23 January 1947

Cheltenham suffered a 5–1 defeat at Gloucester City, with Vernon Crowe scoring the Robins' consolation strike.

23 January 2002

Steve Book made his 250th start for Cheltenham and kept clean sheet in a 0–0 home draw with Darlington.

24 January 1992

Ally Robertson was sacked as Cheltenham boss after a run of 11 Conference games without a victory. His final game in charge ended in a 4–0 defeat by Colchester United.

24 January 1998

Cheltenham lost 2–1 at Northwich Victoria, only their second Saturday defeat of the season after suffering a 3–0 opening day setback at Dover Athletic.

24 January 2006

Cheltenham bowed out of the Football League Trophy at the semi-final stage, going down 1–0 at home to Colchester United with an FA Cup fourth-roundtie at home to Newcastle United looming.

25 January 1986

A crowd of 1,090 watched Cheltenham defeat Barnet 2–1 at Whaddon Road. Mark Boyland – with an exquisite chip over the goalkeeper – and Steve Abbley scored the goals in Cheltenham's first season of Conference football.

25 January 1992

Lindsay Parsons' first home match in charge ended in a 3–2 win over Gateshead, with 2 goals from Jon Purdie and one from local youngster Pete Turnbull.

25 January 1997

Steve Cotterill took control of his first match as caretaker boss, which ended in a 1–0 defeat at Sittingbourne.

25 January 2003

Bobby Gould oversaw his first game in the hot seat for a 0–0 home draw with Chesterfield on the same day long-serving skipper Chris Banks was forced to hang up his boots due to injury.

25 January 2008

John Ward returned to Cheltenham as manager of Carlisle United. Steve Gillespie's goal gave Keith Downing's Robins a 1–0 win – their fourth victory and fourth clean sheet on the trot.

26 January 1980

Two goals in the last fifteen minutes earned Cheltenham a 2–1 win over Taunton Town in the Southern League Midland Division at Whaddon Road. Dave Lewis (from the penalty spot) and John Davies (eight minutes from the end) earned the Robins maximum points.

26 January 2004

Jim Barron was brought back to Cheltenham by manager John Ward to coach goalkeeper Shane Higgs, Steve Book and youth-team number one Craig Humphries.

27 January 1999

Mark Yates completed his transfer from Kidderminster Harriers to Cheltenham Town for a five-figure sum – believed to be £25,000 – equalling the club's then record fee paid for any player.

27 January 2002

Cheltenham claimed one of the biggest FA Cup scalps in their history, stunning Championship club Burnley 2–1 at Whaddon Road in front of more than 7,000 fans. Cheltenham took the game to Burnley right from the off and could have been 2 goals up before Russell Milton's sweetly struck shot, following a clever free-kick move, flew past Luigi Cennamo. Shell-shocked Burnley found themselves two down barely three minutes later. Milton cut inside from the left and his right-footed cross was met by the unchallenged Julian Alsop, who powered his header downwards. As it rose to hit the roof of the net, Whaddon Road erupted. Burnley needed an immediate response and Alan Moore provided it after twenty-nine minutes with a fine individual goal, but Cheltenham saw out the game superbly to move into the last 16, where they would travel to Championship high-fliers West Bromwich Albion. Michael Duff made his 250th start for the club.

28 January 1984

Nick Gazzard scored the Cheltenham goal in a 1–1 draw at home to Folkestone. Cheltenham: Odgen, Murphy, Scarrott, Collicutt, Cornes, Paterson, Berry, Gazzard, Pemberton, Evans, Jordan.

28 January 2003

Grant McCann joined Cheltenham in a club record £50,000 deal on a two-and-a-half-year contract from West Ham United, having been a big hit during loan spells at Whaddon Road.

28 January 2006

Cheltenham hosted Newcastle United in the fourth round of the FA Cup, with the game screened live on *Match of the Day*. A crowd of 7,022 saw the Robins fight bravely before going down 2–0 to the Premier League giants, whose goals came from Michael Chopra and Scott Parker late in the first half. Kayode Odejayi terrorised the Magpies' defence, but wasted a glorious chance to beat Shay Given. John Finnigan was outstanding in the centre of the pitch alongside David Bird, whose wife Nikki was due to give birth to their first child on the day of the big game. Cheltenham: Higgs, Gill, Caines, Townsen, Armstrong, Melligan (Vincent), Finnigan, Bird, Wilson, Odejayi, Guinan (Spencer). Subs not used: Duff, Connolly, Brown.

28 January 2012

Mark Yates' Cheltenham moved to the top of the League Two table with a 3–1 win at Macclesfield Town. The goals at Moss Rose came from Sido Jombati, Jeff Goulding and Luke Garbutt. The match was watched by a crowd of 1,659.

29 January 2011

Leading scorer Wesley Thomas' penalty miss cost
Cheltenham 2 points in a 1–1 draw at Oxford United.
Thomas put the Robins ahead at the Kassam Stadium,
but Tom Craddock levelled.

30 January 1988

Cheltenham crashed to a 5–1 home defeat by
Boston United in the Conference. Mark Buckland
scored the Robins' goal and was one of the few
players to emerge with any credit from the afternoon.
Cheltenham: Churchward, Baverstock, Willetts,
Crowley, Vircavs, Brooks, Buckland, Hughes, B. Angell,
Abbley, Townsend.

30 January 1999

Mark Yates made his Cheltenham Town debut in a 2–0
win at Southport, with goals from Lee Howells and
Neil Grayson.

31 January 1996

Cheltenham lost an FA Trophy first-round second replay
1–0 at Dover Athletic, with Tony Rogers netting the only
goal. Cheltenham: Cook, Wring, Elsey, Banks, Dunphy,
Wright, Howells, Bloomer, Eaton, Waters, Chenoweth.

31 January 1998

Cheltenham beat Rushden & Diamonds 3–1 in the FA Trophy second round to make it one year unbeaten at Whaddon Road. During that time, they won 18 and drew 10 of their 28 fixtures.

31 January 2007

Midfielder Scott Brown suffered a horrific lower leg break in a 1–0 win at Bristol City after an accidental collision with teammate and fellow ex-City man Damian Spencer. Spencer went on to score the only goal of the game at Ashton Gate.

31 January 2009

Damian Spencer fired off a hat-trick in a 5–3 home defeat by Roberto Di Matteo's MK Dons. The front man was swiftly taken off the transfer list by Martin Allen.

FEBRUARY

1 February 1958

Cheltenham thrashed Kidderminster Harriers 9–0, registering their biggest Southern League victory. Peter Cleland and Danny Fowler both scored hat-tricks, with Gordon Workman and Rex Dunlop also on target. The result came a month before they beat Bath City 7–0 and Guildford City 9–1. The team never failed to finish outside the top six of the Southern League between 1954 and 1960 and is considered to be one of the strongest to represent the club in non-league football. The team that faced Kidderminster was: Gourlay, Farrell, Baird, Geddes, Hyde, Dunlop, Carnie, Workman, Cleland, Fowler, Burder.

1 February 1992

Cheltenham got off to the worst possible start in their FA Trophy second-round match at Northwich Victoria, conceding a goal after nine seconds, before a Robins player had touched the ball. Anton Vircavs levelled, but Northwich scored three more before Steve Owen's late consolation made it 4–2.

1 February 2003

Cheltenham drew 0–0 at eventual Division Two (League One) champions Wigan Athletic in Bobby Gould's second match at the helm. Gould switched his full-backs, with Jamie Victory moving into the unfamiliar role of right-back so Antony Griffin could use his pace to combat the threat of Wigan winger Gary Teale.

2 February 1991

Paul Mortimore made his debut for Cheltenham Town at the age of sixteen and scored in a 2–0 FA Trophy second-round victory at Dartford Town.

3 February 1973

Cheltenham drew 0–0 at home with Grantham Town, with Malcolm Crosby making his debut for the club in front of a crowd of 887. Crosby went on to manage Sunderland, leading them to the 1992 FA Cup final, where they lost 2–0 to Liverpool.

3 February 2001

Michael Duff made his 200th Cheltenham Town start in a 1–0 home defeat by Hull City.

4 February 1933

Cheltenham beat South West Ham 8–2 in a friendly match, with Knight scoring five. Evans, Collins and Gough were the other scorers.

4 February 2003

Bobby Gould celebrated his first win as Cheltenham boss 3–1 at home to Tranmere Rovers courtesy of goals from Marvin Brown, Martin Devaney and Tony Naylor.

5 February 1936

Cheltenham Town lost 3–1 to Bristol Rovers Reserves at Eastville, with Edwards scoring the Robins' only goal.

6 February 1988

Darren Angell scored on his Robins debut in a 1–1 home draw with Northwich Victoria.

6 February 1999

Striker Jason Eaton was sent off in an FA Trophy tie against Stevenage after an altercation with ex-Robins back-up goalkeeper Chris Taylor, who was also given his marching orders.

7 February 1995

The usually reliable Jimmy Smith missed from the penalty spot as Cheltenham bowed out of the Dr Marten's League Cup at the quarter-final stage at home against Waterlooville. It was their first appearance in the last 8 of the competition since 1984/85.

8 February 1999

Big defender Mark Freeman scored a wonder goal in the snow at Stevenage in an FA Trophy tie at Broadhall Way, but the match was abandoned due to some brooms which went 'missing', much to the disgust of everyone concerned with Cheltenham Town.

9 February 1999

Young Tewkesbury-based forward Gareth Hopkins scored twice for Cheltenham in a 2–1 Endsleigh Trophy win over Hayes at Whaddon Road.

9 February 2008

Alex Russell and Steven Gillespie both scored in a 2–1 home victory over Brighton & Hove Albion, the vital goals in Cheltenham's battle against the drop from League One coming in the 91st and 94th minutes.

10 February 2003

Cheltenham's record signing, Grant McCann, was called into the Northern Ireland squad for a friendly against Finland in Belfast. The twenty-two-year-old had 5 caps at the time and he replaced Kevin Horlock, who withdrew from the squad. McCann joined teammate Michael Duff in the Northern Ireland camp. They lost the match 1–0 two days later.

11 February 1984

Steve Cotterill made his Cheltenham Town debut as a substitute against Fisher Athletic. He went on to score 7 goals in 20 starts and 13 substitute appearances during his first spell with his hometown club.

11 February 1997

Steve Cotterill picked up his first victory as Cheltenham Town manager after back-to-back defeats by Sittingbourne and Kings Lynn. The result ended Halesowen's 11-match unbeaten run, with Keith Knight scoring at both ends. Lee Howells scored Cheltenham's other goal. Julian Alsop made his final appearance for Halesowen before joining Bristol Rovers.

12 February 1980

A crowd of 89 watched Bedworth beat Cheltenham 2–0 at the Bedworth Oval in the Southern League Midland Division. Cheltenham: Miles, Humphries (Brinkworth), Edwards, Davies, Hams, Dangerfield, Higgins, Hardcastle, Lewis, Reed, Buckland.

12 February 1987

Cheltenham bowed out of the FA Trophy 3–2 at the hands of eventual winners Kidderminster Harriers in front of 3,569 supporters. Mark Boyland and Brian Hughes (penalty) were the Robins' scorers at Whaddon Road. Cheltenham: Hards, Hughes, Willetts, Collicutt (Cotterill), Vircavs, Brooks, Brown, Townsend, Boyland, Baverstock, Jordan (Powell).

12 February 1995

Striker Paul Mortimore left to join Clevedon, with full-back Steve Benton moving in the opposite direction.

13 February 2000

Lee Howells made his 350th Cheltenham Town start against Swansea City, becoming the first player since Kevin Willetts to reach the milestone. He joined Roger Thorndale, Dave Lewis, Joe Hyde, Alan Jefferies and Bill Gourlay in the select group. Loan forward Chris Freestone made his debut in the same match, with Neil Grayson making his 100th start, during which time he scored 42 goals.

14 February 2001

Chris Iwelumo scored on his debut for Cheltenham on loan from Stoke City, but it was not enough to stop them going down 2–1 at Mansfield Town.

14 February 1989

Target man Brett Angell joined Derby County for a fee of £45,000 after scoring 25 goals in 39 appearances for the Robins.

14 February 1995

Cheltenham were beaten 3–1 at non-league giants Woking in the FA Trophy second round, with Neil Smith netting their consolation goal.

14 February 1998

Cheltenham Town's Conference fixture at home to Stevenage was delayed by an hour due to a bomb scare at Whaddon Road. The ground was evacuated and the majority of the crowd ended up watching ex-Robins favourite Mark Buckland in action in a Northern Senior League fixture for Crescent United on Whaddon Recreation Ground.

14 February 2004

John Brough headed in his first goal for nearly a year as Cheltenham beat Boston 1–0 at Whaddon Road.

15 February 1958

Free-scoring Cheltenham beat Merthyr Tydfil 9–1 at home, with Danny Fowler scoring 4 goals and Peter Cleland 3. Rex Dunlop and Clive Burder were also on the scoresheet.

15 February 1992

Scottish poacher Jimmy Smith made his Robins debut at Barrow and went on to become the second-highest scorer in the club's history.

15 February 1997

Bob Bloomer was forced to don the gloves and finish the match in goal due to an injury to Ryan Gannaway as Cheltenham defeated Chelmsford City 1–0 at Whaddon Road. Darren Wright scored the only goal of the game.

15 February 1999

Cheltenham's FA Trophy fourth-roundreplay at Stevenage ended goalless, but Steve Cotterill's side won the replay 5–4 on penalties. Neil Grayson, Clive Walker, Dale Watkins, Bob Bloomer and David Norton all successfully converted from 12 yards, with Michael Love missing for the home side.

16 February 2002

Cheltenham Town's best ever FA Cup run was ended in the fifth round at West Bromwich Albion. More than 5,000 Robins fans made the trip to the Black Country to cheer on their team, who lost out to Danny Dichio's goal. Jamie Victory went agonisingly close to scoring for Cheltenham. Cheltenham: Book, Griffin, Banks, M. Duff, Victory, Williams (Devaney), Howells, Yates, Milton (Brough), Alsop, Naylor (Grayson).

16 February 2008

Cheltenham Town's 400th Football League match was a 1–1 draw against Hartlepool United, with Andy Lindegaard the scorer of their goal.

17 February 2001

Ten-man Cheltenham shocked promotion-chasing Brighton & Hove Albion with a 3–1 victory at Whaddon Road. The goals came from Grant McCann, Julian Alsop and, most memorably, Bob Bloomer, who celebrated as though Cheltenham had won the FA Cup with a jubilant lap of honour. Lee Howells had been sent off after twenty minutes for a second yellow card, which was actually given for a foul by Martin Devaney and the decision was later overturned after a review of the match video. Mark Yates made his 100th start in the same game as Cheltenham ended a winless run of 5 games in fine style. Cheltenham: Book, Griffin, Walker, Howarth, Freeman, McCann, Howells, Yates, Devaney, McAuley, Alsop. (Subs used: Bloomer, White.)

18 February 1995

Kevin Bartley scored in his one and only appearance for Cheltenham Town in a 2–1 home win over Sittingbourne at Whaddon Road in the Premier Division of the Southern League. Steve Benton also made his debut.

18 February 1997

Goalkeeper Jon Skeen made his only first-team appearance for Cheltenham Town in a 4–1 win at Cambridge City. He followed in the footsteps of his father Ken, who played for the club in the 1970s. Jimmy Smith scored twice, with Martin Boyle and Mark Freeman also contributing to the final score.

19 February 1994

Matt Lovell scored a spectacular long-range goal in a 3–1 victory at big-spending promotion rivals Sittingbourne. Bob Bloomer and Jason Eaton were Cheltenham's other scorers at Central Park.

20 February 1999

Cheltenham Town won 2–0 at Hereford United, with goals from Mark Freeman and Jamie Victory. They would have to wait until 2012 for another win over their local rivals. Ex-Bulls midfielder David Norton was subjected to terrible abuse from the home crowd, who spat and threw coins at him, but he had the last laugh, providing the cross from a corner for Victory's clincher.

21 February 1981

Cheltenham failed to break down struggling Wellingborough Town in the Southern League Midland Division, with the match finishing goalless in front of 507 fans at Whaddon Road. Cheltenham: Latchford, Bayliffe, Dyer, Ollis, Boxall, Kavanagh, MacKenzie, Tester, Green, Gardner, Hardcastle.

21 February 1988

David Mogg joined Cheltenham Town from Bath City for a then club record fee of £10,000.

21 February 1989

Cheltenham lost 2–0 at Telford United in the Conference. The result came as part of a poor run of 8 games without a win which plunged the team close to the drop zone. Cheltenham: Churchward, Baverstock, Burns, Craig, Vircavs, Whelan, Brooks, Shearer, Crowley, Buckland, Jordan.

21 February 2009

Cheltenham lost 2–0 at Leeds United, with Michael Antonio forced to leave the pitch with an injury in the 28th minute, having made a promising start on the first appearance of his loan spell from Reading. Both of Leeds' goals were scored by Jonny Howson and the match was watched by a crowd of 20,131.

22 February 1997

Cheltenham went down 2–0 at Gresley Rovers, who put themselves firmly on course for the Dr Marten's League title, but their Moat Street ground was not up to Conference requirements, so Cheltenham knew that the runners-up spot would be enough to earn a return to non-league football's top echelon. Cheltenham: Gannaway, Wotton, Symonds, Banks, Freeman, Victory, Howells, Wright, Boyle, Smith, Bloomer.

23 February 1952

Bishop's Cleeve-based defender Joe Hyde made his debut in a 1–0 home win over Yeovil Town. His final appearance was against Chelmsford City in March 1961, by which time he had chalked up more than 400 for the club.

23 February 1985

Cheltenham lost a top-of-the-table clash 2–1 to Kings Lynn, with Brian Hughes on target for the Robins, who recovered to pip their opponents to the title that season. Cheltenham: Moss, Boxall, Scarrott, Collicutt, Cornes, Goff, Hughes, Abbley, Boyland, Cotterill, Hacker.

24 February 1988

Graham Withey scored on his Cheltenham Town debut in a 2–2 Conference draw against Maidstone United.

24 February 1997

Jimmy Wring left Cheltenham to join Newport AFC.

24 February 1999

Defender Neil Howarth joined Cheltenham from League Two Macclesfield Town for a fee of £7,500, rising to £10,000 if the club were successful in their Conference title push.

25 February 1992

The prolific Jimmy Smith scored his first goals for Cheltenham Town in a 3–1 win at Slough Town.

26 February 1968

Bob Etheridge's Cheltenham side thrashed Barnet 4–0 at home, with Joe Gadston scoring all of the goals before a crowd of 2,099.

26 February 1977

Dave Lewis was the only Cheltenham scorer as their promotion hopes took a severe blow at Kidderminster Harriers, who ran out 4–1 winners. Cheltenham were promoted as runners-up to Worcester City.

26 February 1997

RAF man Garry Wotton left Cheltenham to sign for Hayes.

27 February 1937

Cheltenham were beaten 6–0 by Chelsea in a friendly match at Whaddon Road.

27 February 1993

Cheltenham's hopes of bouncing back to the Conference evaporated with a 2–0 defeat at Dorchester Town. Cheltenham: Nicholls, Lovell, Willetts, Brown, Vircavs, Owen, Howells, N. Smith, J. Smith, Iddles, Bloomer.

27 February 2004

Mark Yates rejoined Kidderminster Harriers, having been released by Cheltenham. The thirty-four-year-old made 233 starts for the Robins, scoring 22 goals. He helped Kidderminster avoid relegation from the Football League with 14 appearances and 2 goals before embarking on his coaching career at Burnley, where he was number two to Steve Cotterill.

28 February 1990

Former Everton and Scotland star Andy Gray made his final Cheltenham appearance in a 3–0 FA Trophy replay defeat by Kingstonian. The first match finished 3–3. Cheltenham: Churchward, Burns, Crowley, Vircavs, Willetts, Williams, Brooks, Buckland, Jordan, Boyland (Nuttell), Gray.

29 February 1992

Cheltenham suffered one of their heaviest-ever home defeats, going down 7–0 to Redbridge Forest in a Conference clash watched by 909 disbelieving supporters.

MARCH

1 March 2001

Steve Cotterill described defender Chris Banks as Cheltenham Town's 'greatest ever player' after his quick return from injury helped kick-start the Robins' play-off bid. Banks had undergone knee surgery, but returned just twelve days later.

2 March 2012

Mark Yates agreed a two-year extension to his contract as Cheltenham Town manager, along with his assistant Neil Howarth.

2 March 1986

Second-half goals from Steve Abbley and recent signing John Powell saw Cheltenham to a 2–0 win over Barrow in the Conference. Cheltenham: Hards, Hughes, Baddeley, Aizlewood, Cornes, Brooks, Willetts, Baverstock, Boyland, Abbley, Powell.

2 March 1999

Mark Yates, Neil Grayson, Steve Book and Dale Watkins all played for John Owens' England semi-professional team in a 4–1 win over Italy at Hayes' Church Road ground. Grayson scored twice. Vincenzo Iaquinta scored for Italy; he went on to play for Juventus and win 40 caps for the full Azzurri side.

3 March 1982

Steve Scarrott scored Cheltenham's goal in a 1–1 home draw with Redditch United in the Southern League Midland Division. Only 248 fans were present at Whaddon Road. Cheltenham: Harris, Buckland, Dyer, Boxall, Bayliffe, Scarrott, Reed, MacKenzie, Pemberton, Shatford, Tester.

3 March 1990

Goals either side of half-time from Mark Buckland and Simon Brain, a young striker signed from Evesham United, helped Cheltenham beat Sutton United 2–0 in the Conference. It was a welcome morale booster after the recent FA Trophy defeat by Kingstonian and the subsequent departure of Andy Gray. Cheltenham: Churchward, Whelan, Willetts, Crowley, Vircavs, Burns, Brooks, Nuttell, Brain, Buckland, Purdie.

3 March 1998

Chris Banks, Lee Howells, Neil Grayson and Dale Watkins all started for the England semi-professional side against Holland, with Jamie Victory also going on as a substitute, causing the Robins fans in the crowd at Crawley Town's Broadfield Stadium to chant: 'It's just like watching Cheltenham.' Grayson and Halifax's Mark Bradshaw scored the goals in a 2–1 win, with Watkins named man of the match on a proud night for the club.

4 March 2006

Goals from Gavin Caines and Steven Gillespie earned John Ward's Cheltenham a 2–1 home win over Wycombe Wanderers, strengthening their play-off push.

5 March 1988

Cheltenham were knocked out of the FA Trophy in the quarter-finals 4–2 by Telford United, with Mark Buckland and Darren Angell the scorers. It was their best run in the competition until 1998, when they won it for the first and only time.

5 March 2002

Lee Howells broke his fibula and tibia at the club he played for as a youngster, Bristol Rovers. It was due to an innocuous challenge with Latvian Vitālijs Astafjevs. Cheltenham won the match 2–1 with goals from Richard Walker and Julian Alsop, but Howells' season was over and Steve Cotterill moved quickly to bring in John Finnigan from Lincoln City as his replacement.

6 March 1999

Mark Freeman was sent off in a 1–1 Conference draw at Barrow, with Keith Knight the scorer of Cheltenham's goal.

6 March 2004

John Ward's Cheltenham side snatched a thrilling victory from the jaws of defeat in an enthralling contest at Whaddon Road against Lincoln City. Grant McCann, ex-Imps skipper John Finnigan and Kayode Odejayi were the Robins' scorers, with the last two coming in the 87th and 90th minutes to make it 3–2 to the home side. Cheltenham: Higgs, Griffin (Gill), M. Duff, Brough, Victory, Devaney, Finnigan, Forsyth (Cleverley), McCann, Spencer, Brayson (Odejayi). Subs not used: Book, Bird.

7 March 1987

Steve Cotterill made his third start since recovering from a serious knee injury in an away game at Gateshead. He partnered Mark Boyland up front and it was Boyland who scored the Robins' goal in a 1–1 draw. Cheltenham: Hards, Baverstock, Willetts, Crowley, Vircavs, Brooks, Brown, Hughes, Boyland, Cotterill, Townsend.

7 March 1995

Cheltenham stayed hot on the heels of leaders Hednesford Town with a 4–1 win at Gresley Rovers. Christer Warren, who earned a big-money move to Southampton a few weeks later, scored the opening 2 goals and there were further strikes from Jimmy Smith and Lee Howells. Cheltenham: Thomas, Howells, Howell, Banks, Jones, N. Smith, Warren, Cooper, J. Smith, Boyle, Benton.

7 March 1998

Neil Grayson made his debut in a 4–1 defeat at Rushden & Diamonds as Cheltenham were reduced to nine men, with both Mark Freeman and Keith Knight sent off.

7 March 2011

Cheltenham Reserves beat Gloucester City 5–2 in the Gloucestershire Senior Cup.

8 March 1952

Cheltenham suffered a club record 10–1 defeat by Merthyr Tydfil in the Southern League.

8 March 1958

Cheltenham beat Guildford City 9–1, with goals from Carnie, Cleland, Fowler, Dunlop and Scott. They scored 51 goals in 12 matches between January and March that year, including 7–0 v. Bath, 9–0 v. Kidderminster Harriers and 9–1 v. Merthyr Tydfil in three epic home victories.

8 March 2003

Shane Higgs was given a chance to impress in goal after three-and-a-half years as number two to Steve Book in a match against Mansfield Town. Cheltenham won 3–1 with goals from Martin Devaney,

Marvin Brown and Damian Spencer. Higgs went on to become number one for more than five years, twice winning the Supporters' Player of the Year award.

9 March 1983

Cheltenham raced into a 2–0 lead in the Southern League Cup semi-final second leg against Alvechurch at Whaddon Road. Trailing 1–0 from the first leg, goals from Terry Paterson and Gary Stevens improved their position, but Alvechurch hit back to draw 2–2 and reach the final. Cheltenham: Ogden, Ryan, Scarrott, Murphy, Cornes, Paterson, Secker, Stevens, Jones, Pemberton, Tester.

9 March 1989

Mark Boyland returned to Cheltenham from Aylesbury United.

9 March 1999

One goal for Jamie Victory and one against his old club by John Brough earned Cheltenham a 2–2 home draw with Hereford United. Both Hereford's goals came from ex-Cheltenham man John Brough. Robins fans were disappointed not to take 3 points against their local rivals, but the draw proved another valuable point towards claiming the Conference crown. Cheltenham: Book, Duff, Victory, Brough, Freeman, R. Walker, Yates, Bloomer, Grayson, Eaton, Knight.

9 March 2002

John Finnigan scored on his debut in a 4–0 home win over York City, Cheltenham's biggest Football League win to that date.

10 March 1951

Cheltenham beat Portsmouth 8–0 in a friendly, with Roy Shiner and Norman Mills scoring hat-tricks. Sabbatella Sabbatella and Vernon Crowe were the other scorers.

10 March 1976

Dave Lewis scored 4 goals in a 6–0 win over Stevenage Athletic, with Dave Dangerfield and Colin Hall the other scorers in front of a crowd of 295.

10 March 1979

Cheltenham slipped to a 1–0 defeat by AP Leamington in the Southern League Premier Division. The team was in the middle of a poor run, with one win in 11 games, sending them into the bottom half of the table and out of the race to qualify for the newly formed Alliance Premier League the following season. Cheltenham: Miles, Murphy, Dangerfield, Foster, Dean, MacKenzie, Lewis, Fleet, Payne, Davies, Bayliffe.

10 March 2007

Hungarian international Denes Rosa made his Cheltenham debut in a 2–1 home defeat by Yeovil Town. He was on loan from Wolves and appeared four times for John Ward's team.

11 March 1989

Mark Boyland scored 4 goals on his return to Cheltenham's team in a 4–1 win at Chorley, witnessed by a crowd of 620. It was their first away win for three months. He went on to score 8 goals in 11 games that season. His goals came in the 45th, 53rd, 65th and 70th minutes, with the last two from the penalty spot. Cheltenham: Churchward, Baverstock, Crowley, Vircavs (Craig), Willetts, Jordan, Whelan, Burns, Buckland, Boyland, Nuttell. Sub: Crouch.

11 March 1995

Cheltenham beat title rivals Hednesford Town 2–0 at
Whaddon Road thanks to goals from Martin Boyle and
Jimmy Smith. A bumper crowd of 2,031 – their highest
in over a year – assembled and Cheltenham needed
a win to keep the pressure on their visitors, who
were threatening to runaway with the championship.
Smith's corner was cleared to the edge of the penalty
area, where Boyle was waiting. After his first shot
was blocked, he calmly placed the ball into the bottom
corner to give Cheltenham the initiative in the 6th
minute. Hednesford full-back Kevin Collins was sent
off after an altercation with Simon Cooper, when a
punch appeared to be thrown as the pair wrestled on
the ground. The match was played in wet conditions
and the pitch was muddy, but Cheltenham played some
fine football. Skipper Neil Smith sustained a cut to his
face early in the second half and he had to be virtually
dragged off the pitch, such was his desire to continue
in the engine room. Cheltenham doubled their lead in
the 52nd minute through Jimmy Smith's brilliant free-
kick after Chris Banks had been tripped on the edge of
the box. Cheltenham: Thomas, Benton (Eaton), Howell,
Banks, Jones, N. Smith (Wring), Howells, Cooper,
J. Smith, Boyle, Warren. Sub (not used): Cook.

11 March 2008

Goals from David Bird and Alex Russell earned Cheltenham a famous victory at the once mighty Leeds United's Elland Road in front of 20,257 supporters. Bristol City loanee Richard Keogh made his debut and was outstanding alongside the equally excellent Shane Duff at centre-half. Steve Brooker missed a good chance to make it 3–0 to Cheltenham before Anthony Elding pulled one back for Leeds in the 85th minute. It was a fully deserved success for Keith Downing's men. Cheltenham: Higgs, Gill, Keogh, Duff, Wright, Gillespie, Bird, Russell, Armstrong, Spencer (Vincent), Brooker (Connor). Subs not used: Brown, Lindegaard, D'Agostino.

12 March 1892

Cheltenham Town took on Dean Close School in a friendly and lost 4–3 in Prestbury. It is one of the earliest recorded matches in the club's history.

12 March 1986

Cheltenham reached the quarter-finals of the FA Trophy for the first time in their history, but they were knocked out 2–0 by eventual winners Altrincham.

12 March 2002

Cheltenham registered their 7th consecutive away win at Lincoln City with Julian Alsop netting the decisive goal to make the final score 1–0.

12 March 2003

Damian Spencer scored a memorable long-range goal as Cheltenham stunned Swindon Town 3–0 at the County Ground. Martin Devaney and John Brough were the other scorers.

13 March 1999

Cheltenham preserved their 7-match unbeaten run with a 2–2 draw at Stevenage, despite having Bob Bloomer sent off for two yellow cards.

13 March 2004

Mark Yates made his final start for Cheltenham Town, scoring in a 3–1 home win over Doncaster Rovers.

13 March 2010

Cheltenham Town staged one of the most remarkable comebacks in Football League history to stun Burton Albion 6–5 at the Pirelli Stadium. Michael Pook was the hero, scoring a hat-trick within ten minutes as Mark Yates' side hit back from 2–0, 4–2 and 5–3 down to snatch an amazing win. It was the first time any side had won 6–5 away from home in a Football League game since Manchester United defeated Chelsea by the odd goal in eleven in 1954. The last team to win a League fixture 6–5 were Grimsby Town, who edged out Burnley in October 2002.

14 March 1979

A meagre crowd of 225 turned out to watch
Cheltenham draw 1–1 with Maidstone United –
the club's lowest ever Southern League crowd.
The average that season at Whaddon Road was 531.

14 March 1998

Cheltenham reached the semi-finals of the FA Trophy
for the first time by beating Hayes 1–0 in an ill-
tempered encounter at Whaddon Road. Jamie Victory
scored the winner after a free-kick was awarded as a
result of Hayes goalkeeper Russell Meara taking too
many steps with the ball in his hands. A fight broke out
between Hayes substitutes and Cheltenham fans in the
paddock area.

15 March 2008

Cheltenham edged to a 1–0 League One home
win over Bristol Rovers, thanks to a goal from
Steve Brooker.

16 March 1985

Cheltenham enjoyed a 5–1 win over Crawley Town,
with goals from Nick Jordan (2), Ray Baverstock,
Mark Hacker and an own goal.

16 March 1993

Anton Vircavs made his 300th appearance for Cheltenham Town in a 1–1 home draw with Dover Athletic. Bob Bloomer scored the Robins' goal in front of a crowd of 1,159. Vircavs made his 301st and final appearance against Solihull Borough four days later, before joining Wycombe Wanderers.

16 March 1999

Dennis Bailey joined Cheltenham from Farnborough Town on a two-year deal and made his debut in a 0–0 home draw against his former club, with Lee Howells making his 300th start.

16 March 2002

Steve Book was sent off for the first time in his career in a 4–1 defeat for Cheltenham at struggling Halifax Town. Jamie Victory scored their only goal at The Shay and goalkeeper Shane Higgs made his second Robins Football League appearance as a substitute after Book's dismissal.

17 March 2001

Cheltenham staged their own mini goal of the season competition in a 4–2 home win over Halifax Town. Mark Yates and Gregory Goodridge scored the most spectacular of the strikes, with Neil Grayson and Russell Milton the other scorers. Charlie MacDonald and Mark Sertori both made their debuts.

17 March 2004

Cheltenham lost 1–0 at Oxford United, whose squad included former Robins striker Julian Alsop. The only goal was a penalty from Andy Crosby.

18 March 2006

Brian Wilson earned Cheltenham a 1–0 win at Chester City in League Two.

19 March 1983

Cheltenham Town lost 2–1 at home to Merthyr in the Southern League Midland Division. Paul Tester, scorer of the Robins' only goal, ended the season with 25 goals as the Robins finished a point clear of Sutton Coldfield Town at the top of the table.

20 March 1999

Cheltenham won a top-of-the-table Conference clash against Kettering Town 3–0, with 2 own goals helping their cause and the outstanding Neil Grayson on target. Cheltenham returned to the top of the table after a sixteen-week absence. The match was watched by 5,202, Cheltenham's highest league attendance on record at that time.

21 March 1992

Richard Clark and Christer Warren made their debuts in a 1–1 draw at Farnborough Town, with Kevin Willetts netting an 87th-minute equaliser for Lindsay Parsons' team.

21 March 2000

Wrexham loan front man Ian Stevens made his only appearance for Cheltenham in a 2–1 home win over Northampton Town. He hit the post, but goals from Michael Duff and Jamie Victory were enough to earn Cheltenham an impressive victory.

22 March 1980

Cheltenham visited Kidderminster Harriers for a Southern League Midland Division fixture, looking to improve on a lower mid-table position. However, Harriers proved too strong and claimed a 3–1 victory, with Chris Gardner on target for the Robins. Cheltenham: Miles, Davies, Edwards, Humphries, Hams, Brinkworth, Rice, Higgins, Lewis, Gardner, Hardcastle.

22 March 1997

Cheltenham hit back to earn a 3–3 draw at home to Burton Albion after some calamitous goalkeeping from Ryan Gannaway. Chris Banks, Jimmy Smith and Jamie Victory were the scorers after Gannaway was at fault for all three of the Brewers' goals. Cheltenham: Gannaway, Clarke, Knight, Banks, Chenoweth, Victory, Howells, Wright, Dunwell, Smith, Bloomer.

22 March 2002

Promising speed merchant Nathan Tyson joined Cheltenham Town on loan from Reading.

23 March 1976

Pat Casey broke his leg at Merthyr Tydfil after a collision with the goalkeeper. He recovered from the horrific injury and played for another four years, but he was never quite the same. Casey scored 68 goals in 231 games for Cheltenham, most of which were at outside right. He was signed by Bob Etheridge at the age of eighteen in 1969, but was nineteen by the time the season started. He spent a decade at the club, setting up many of Dave Lewis' goals in that period. Cheltenham: N. Berry, Murphy, Lailey, McLaughlin, Davies, Collicutt, Dangerfield, Casey, Hehir, Skeen, Hall.

23 March 1985

Defender Stuart Cornes pounced upon a goalkeeping error in the first half to put Cheltenham 1–0 up against Welling United in the Southern League Premier Division at Whaddon Road. The Kent club equalised in the second half, but the result proved a valuable point towards the championship at the end of the season. Cheltenham: Moss, Murphy, Scarrott, Boxall, Cornes, Abbley, Hughes, Baverstock, Boyland, Hacker, Jordan.

23 March 1993

Anton Vircavs left to sign for Wycombe Wanderers and Cheltenham lost 2–1 on their first visit to Halesowen Town since 1935. Lee Howells scored their goal. Cheltenham: Nicholls, Lovell, Wring, Brown, Howells, Cooper, Warren, N. Smith, J. Smith, Eaton, Bloomer.

23 March 1996

Cheltenham's faint hopes of catching runaway leaders Rushden & Diamonds were extinguished by a 2–1 home defeat by their nemeses, Hastings Town. The Sussex club won at Whaddon Road for the second time in four years. Jason Eaton scored a late consolation goal in a 2–1 defeat. Cheltenham Town: Goodwin, Wotton, Benton, Banks, Freeman, Elsey, Bloomer, Wright, Eaton, Smith, Chenoweth.

24 March 1984

A penalty from Ray Baverstock seven minutes from full-time rescued a point for Cheltenham Town at home to Gravesend & Northfleet in the Southern League Premier Division. The result made it 1 defeat in 9 for the Robins, who climbed back to a mid-table position in their first season back in the Premier Division. The match was also the full first team debut of Steve Cotterill. Cheltenham: Ogden, Murphy, Scarrott, Collicutt, Cornes, Paterson, D. Berry, Baverstock, Cotterill, Evans, Jordan.

24 March 1992

Cheltenham Town achieved a rare home win during an unhappy season that saw them suffer relegation from the Conference. Telford United were the visitors, and second-half goals by defenders Richard Clark and Kevin Willetts earned a 2–1 victory. Cheltenham: Nicholls, Howells, Willetts, Clark, Brooks, N. Smith, Brogan, Owen, J. Smith, Bloomfield, Purdie.

24 March 2009

Kyle Haynes made his Cheltenham Town debut as a substitute against Oldham Athletic, becoming the club's youngest Football League player at seventeen years, two months and twenty-six days.

25 March 1989

Struggling Weymouth visited Whaddon Road and took a surprise lead in the Conference clash. Big central defender Anton Vircavs headed an equaliser eighteen minutes from the end. Cheltenham: Churchward, Willetts, Burns, Crowley, Vircavs, Baverstock, Brooks, Boyland, Nuttell, Buckland, Jordan.

25 March 1997

Chris Banks made his 150th Cheltenham appearance in a 2–2 draw with Gresley Rovers.

25 March 1998

Cheltenham suffered their first home defeat in 30 games, with old adversary Paul Davies netting the only goal for Kidderminster Harriers.

25 March 2000

Cheltenham moved into the Division Three play-off places for the first time with a 2–1 win at Exeter City, thanks to goals from Jamie Victory and Martin Devaney.

26 March 1977

A crowd of 1,096 gathered for the top of the table Southern League Division One (North) meeting between Cheltenham Town and Bromsgrove Rovers at Whaddon Road. With Worcester City clear at the top, the match was one of the key battles for second place and Cheltenham were disappointed to lose 1–0, but they did eventually grab second spot. Cheltenham: Miles, Murphy, Edwards, Foster, Dean, Paterson, Rice, Dangerfield, Davies, Lewis, Price.

26 March 1988

England semi-professional international Steve Brooks scored for Cheltenham after half an hour as they drew 1–1 at the Wessex Stadium, home of Weymouth. This was a good result for the team, as Weymouth had been among the strongest team in the Conference that season. Keith Knight made his full Cheltenham Town debut in the game. Cheltenham: Mogg, Hughes, Willetts, Baverstock, Crowley, Brooks, Buckland, Knight, Withey, Abbley, Jordan.

26 March 2002

Nathan Tyson and Tony Naylor's goals earned Cheltenham a 2–1 home win over Kidderminster Harriers in what proved to be Chris Banks' final appearance due to a career-ending knee injury.

27 March 1999

Neil Howarth's first goal for Cheltenham in the 44th minute took them safely through to the FA Trophy semi-finals for the second year in succession in a 1–0 win at Emley. It was their 100th FA Trophy tie. Cheltenham: Book, Knight (Casey), Victory, Banks, Freeman, Howarth, Howells, Milton, Grayson, Eaton, Norton.

28 March 1981

Goals at either end of the game from John Dyer and local youngster Andy Winkett sealed a 2–0 win over Witney Town. The result came during a then club record 22-game unbeaten League run. Cheltenham: Latchford, Bayliffe, Dyer, Ollis, Boxall, Kavanagh, MacKenzie, Tester, Green, Pemberton, Hardcastle.

28 March 1992

Cheltenham drew 1–1 at home to Boston United, with Marc Coates scoring two minutes into his debut. Mark Davies and Charlie Henry also made their first Cheltenham appearances.

28 March 1998

Cheltenham hit back from a goal down to beat Dover 2–1 at Whaddon Road in the first leg of their FA Trophy semi-final, with Jason Eaton scoring both goals. It was Chris Banks' 200th appearance.

29 March 1997

Cheltenham recovered from a goal down to win 5–1 at Halesowen Town in a result pivotal to their 1997 Southern League promotion success. Mark Freeman's own goal gave the Yeltz the lead, but strikes from Keith Knight, Richard Dunwell, Darren Wright and Martin Boyle completed an emphatic comeback in front of 1,406 spectators. Cheltenham: Maloy, Chenoweth (Eaton), Knight, Banks, Freeman, Victory, Howells, Wright, Dunwell, Boyle, Bloomer. Other subs: Duff, Cotterill.

30 March 1999

Steve Book and Neil Grayson won England caps against Holland at Sportclub Genemuiden in a 1–1 draw.

30 March 2004

Brian Wilson joined Cheltenham for a club record-equalling fee of £50,000 from Stoke City on a three-year contract.

31 March 1961

Joe Hyde made his final appearance for Cheltenham Town in a 2–2 draw with Chelmsford City.

31 March 1964

Bob Etheridge joined Cheltenham Town from Bristol City. He went on to manage the club from 1966 to 1973.

31 March 1986

Two goals in three minutes before half-time earned Cheltenham an impressive 2–0 home win over Altrincham. John Powell and Kevin Willetts were the scorers. Cheltenham: Hards, Hughes, Baddeley, Baverstock, Cornes, Brooks, Willetts, Townsend, Boyland, Abbley, Powell.

31 March 1990

Goals from Mark Buckland and a Kevin Willetts penalty put Cheltenham 2–0 up at home to Runcorn, but the Merseyside team hit back to earn a 2–2 draw. Cheltenham: Churchward, Crowley, Willetts, Baverstock, Purdie, Williams, Brooks, Nuttell, Brain, Buckland, Jordan.

31 March 1997

Bitter rivals Cheltenham Town and Gloucester City drew 1–1 at Whaddon Road in the race for the runners-up spot behind Gresley Rovers in the Southern League Premier Division. It was watched by 3,005 fans – Cheltenham's highest crowd for a league match since 3,015 watched them play Atherstone Town in April 1973. Darren Wright headed in the leveller for Cheltenham after Leroy Rosenior's men took the lead. It was Cheltenham's final Southern League meeting with their old rivals, and they ended with an impressive record. They ended the season with 36 wins from 64 matches, having lost 10 and drawn 18. Their final goal tally was 132 for and 74 against.

31 March 1998

Cheltenham, possibly distracted by their involvement in the FA Trophy semi-finals, were held to a 0–0 draw at Telford United in the Conference. The match took place in the middle of Cheltenham's two-legged last four clash with Dover Athletic. Cheltenham: Book, Duff, Victory, Banks, Freeman, Knight, Howells, Milton, Eaton, Grayson, Bloomer.

APRIL

1 April 1972

Cheltenham lost 4–0 to Kettering Town, who included player/manager Ron Atkinson in their line-up. The game was watched by a crowd of 2,111. Kettering went on to win the Southern League Division One (North) title, with Cheltenham third, behind second-placed Burton Albion.

1 April 1975

Dave Lewis scored his 50th goal of the season in a 2–2 draw with Merthyr Tydfil. He finished the campaign with a club record haul of 53.

1 April 1978

A goal four minutes from the end secured Cheltenham Town a point at home in a 1–1 draw against Wealdstone. Manager Denis Allen began the process of giving local youngsters a chance in the Southern League Premier Division with Tim Bayliffe, Nigel Berry and Duncan Berry all given a run out. Cheltenham: N. Berry, Murphy, Dangerfield, Bayliffe, Dean, Paterson, Foster, Brown, Lewis, Bryant, D. Berry.

1 April 1991

Goals from Chris Burton, Anton Vircavs and Derek Payne earned Cheltenham a 3–0 win at Slough Town in the Conference, their third away success of the season.

1 April 2001

Neil Grayson scored a memorable hat-trick in a 3–1 home win over Cardiff City, the fifth treble of his career and his first for Cheltenham at the age of thirty-six. Cheltenham: Book, Walker, Banks, Sertori, McCann, Milton, Yates, Howells, Duff, MacDonald (Alsop), Grayson. Subs not used: Griffin, Higgs, McAuley.

2 April 1994

Cheltenham's hopes of winning the Southern League title took a blow when they drew 2–2 away to John Murphy's Trowbridge Town. A Jimmy Smith penalty and a goal from Jason Eaton put the Robins 2–1 up, but a late strike denied them all 3 points. Cheltenham: Thomas, Bloomer, S. Jones, Clark, N. Smith, Cooper, Howells, Diaz, J. Smith, Eaton, Lovell.

2 April 2011

Cheltenham suffered a humiliating club record Football League defeat, going down 8–1 at Crewe Alexandra. It was the club's heaviest defeat since 1969. Wesley Thomas' strike provided scant consolation for the beleaguered Robins.

3 April 1993

Paul Bloomfield scored his first Cheltenham Town goal in his 55th appearance, netting in a 1–1 draw against Atherstone United.

3 April 1999

Cheltenham hit back from a goal down in the 90th minute to win 2–1 at Rushden & Diamonds, with injury-time goals from substitute Mark Freeman, and Neil Grayson. It was one of the most important and memorable wins in the club's history, putting Steve Cotterill's team in pole position for the Conference title, while Rushden never recovered. Their goal was scored by Miguel de Souza, who made one appearance for Cheltenham at Birmingham in an FA Cup first-round tie. The crowd was 6,312, with hundreds locked outside the stadium. Cheltenham: Book, Duff, Banks, Brough, Howarth (Freeman), Victory, Howells, Bloomer (Milton), Norton, Grayson, Bailey (Knight).

4 April 1978

Cheltenham were beaten 6–0 at home by Bath City. They had beaten Bath 7–1 in the FA Trophy earlier in the season and drawn 4–4 at Twerton Park in the Southern League Premier Division. Cheltenham: N. Berry, Murphy, Dangerfield, Davies, Dean, Foster, Paterson, Brown, Lewis, Bryant, Casey. Sub: D. Berry.

4 April 1998

Cheltenham booked their place at Wembley by drawing the second leg of their FA Trophy semi-final at Dover Athletic. The goals came from Dale Watkins and Jason Eaton in the first half. Neil Le Bihan and John Budden made it interesting with goals in the 70th and 78th minutes respectively, but Cheltenham held on in front of a crowd of 3,240. Cheltenham: Book, Duff, Banks, Freeman, Victory, Milton (Wright), Howells, Walker, Eaton, Watkins, Bloomer.

5 April 1969

Cheltenham went down 1–0 to Cambridge United in the Southern League Cup final first leg.

5 April 1999

Neil Grayson's goal sealed a vital 1–0 home win over Kidderminster Harriers as Cheltenham took another step towards the Conference title and promotion to the Football League for the first time.

5 April 2003

Julian Alsop was sent off for an altercation with Leo Roget in Cheltenham's 2–2 League One draw at Brentford.

5 April 2008

Steven Gillespie gave Cheltenham the lead at Nottingham Forest, but the former European Champions hit back to win 3–1. Alan Wright was given a tremendous ovation by the Forest fans.

6 April 1991

Cheltenham were held to a 0–0 Conference draw by Bath City at Whaddon Road in front of a crowd of 966.

7 April 1979

Terry Paine took charge of his first match as Cheltenham Town manager, which resulted in a 2–0 defeat at Barnet.

7 April 1992

Cheltenham Town beat Gloucester City 4–2 in the Gloucestershire Senior Cup final. Neil Smith suffered a fracture of his cheek, which ruled him out for the rest of the season. The goals came from Marc Coates, Jimmy Smith and Charlie Henry.

7 April 1999

Scout Derek Bragg went on as a substitute in Cheltenham's 2–0 Endsleigh Trophy semi-final defeat at Farnborough Town, becoming the oldest player to represent the club.

8 April 1966

Bob Etheridge was appointed player-manager of Cheltenham Town. He was an accomplished all-round sportsman who played 39 matches for Gloucestershire County Cricket Club. He was player-manager from 1966 until 1973, following a distinguished League career with Bristol City, for whom he played more than 300 times. His final Robins appearance record was 198, during which time he scored 7 goals.

8 April 1996

Two goals from Jason Eaton along with David Elsey's acrobatic strike earned Cheltenham a 3–0 win at rivals Gloucester City. Elsey was later sent off. It was Jimmy Smith's 200th appearance for Cheltenham and he set up two of their goals at Meadow Park. Eaton's double took his tally for the season to 21 and he finished with 26, scooping the manager's, players' and supporters' Player of the Year awards. Kevin Maloy made a string of saves to preserve Cheltenham's clean sheet – he was the sixth goalkeeper used that season, following Martin Thomas, Mark Teasdale, Shane Cook, Mark Davies and Nick Goodwin. Cheltenham: Maloy, Wotton, Benton (Campbell), Banks, Freeman, Elsey, Bloomer, Wring, Eaton, Smith, Chenoweth (Wright). Sub (not used): Parker.

8 April 2000

Martin Devaney's fine individual effort helped Cheltenham to a 2–1 win at Lincoln City. Jamie Victory was their other scorer. Chris Banks became the sixteenth post-war player to pass the 300 appearance mark for Cheltenham at Sincil Bank, while Jamie Victory made his 150th consecutive league appearance, having not missed one since Crawley away in December 1996.

9 April 1977

A 4–0 Easter Saturday victory over Gloucester City helped Cheltenham Town on their way to a runners-up finish in the Southern League Division One North. Dave Lewis scored twice, with John Davies and Tony Price also on target. It was the second of a nine-match unbeaten run to end the campaign.

9 April 1988

Lincoln City's first visit to Whaddon Road ended in a 3–3 draw. Mark Sertori, who went on to play for Cheltenham and is the current Manchester City masseur, was among the Lincoln scorers. Cheltenham's scorers were Kevin Willetts, Anton Vircavs and Nick Jordan, with all the goals coming in the first half.

9 April 2002

Cheltenham's automatic promotion hopes were dented after a 2–1 defeat at Mansfield Town in front of 8,633 supporters. Mark Yates scored Cheltenham's goal, but Steve Cotterill's team had to settle for a play-off place, while Mansfield finished third.

10 April 1975

Goalkeeper Alan Jefferies made his 400th appearance for Cheltenham in a 2–1 home defeat by Redditch United.

10 April 1999

Cheltenham drew 2–2 in the first leg of their FA Trophy semi-final at Kingstonian in a bid to reach Wembley for the second season in succession. The goals came from Neil Grayson and John Brough.

10 April 2010

Winger Josh Low inspired Cheltenham Town to a 5–2 win at home against Bury, scoring twice. Barry Hayles, Matt Thornhill and Justin Richards scored the other goals.

11 April 1964

Cheltenham won a club record ninth match in succession, beating Canterbury City 2–1 with goals from Ron Crichton and Bobby McCool. Cheltenham went on to finish third in Southern League Division One behind Folkestone Town and King's Lynn.

11 April 1987

A goal from Steve Brooks deep into injury time earned Cheltenham a point from their last ever visit to London Road Stadium, former home of Maidstone United. That season brought another mid-table finish for the Robins in the Conference plus a good run in the FA Trophy, while Maidstone geared up for their championship season the following term. Cheltenham: Hards, Baverstock, Willetts, Crowley, Vircavs, Brooks, Brown, Hughes, Boyland, Townsend, Jordan.

11 April 1995

A tremendous performance from Cheltenham saw them win 4–1 at Dorchester Town to keep them on the heels of leaders Hednesford Town. Christer Warren, Martin Boyle, Andy Tucker and Lee Howells scored the goals. Cheltenham: Thomas, Wring, Benton, Banks, Jones, N. Smith, Tucker, J. Smith, Boyle, Warren.

12 April 1969

A goalless draw at home to Cambridge United was not enough to win the two-legged final of the Southern League Cup. They lost 1–0 on aggregate.

12 April 1993

Cheltenham Town thrashed near neighbours Gloucester City 5–1 with goals from Lee Howells, Bob Bloomer, Jason Eaton and Jimmy Smith, making it a very happy Easter for Robins fans. A crowd of 1,072 watched at Meadow Park. Cheltenham scored several times, stretching their lead to 3–0 while they played for half an hour with ten men to City's eleven. They were a man light after the 35th-minute sending-off of Steve Owen for headbutting Shaun Penny at the end of a scuffle which also involved Ray Baverstock, the ex-Robins hardman. Baverstock was sent off himself in the 65th minute when he threw the ball into Neil Smith's face, having already been shown a yellow card. It was 5–0 before Gloucester scrambled their 87th minute goal. Cheltenham: Barrett, Bloomer, N. Smith, Brown, Howells, Owen, Cooper, Iddles, J. Smith (Lovell), Eaton, Bloomfield, Hirons.

12 April 1997

Player-manager Steve Cotterill operated at centre-back in a 1–0 home win over Hastings Town, with Darren Wright netting the only goal of the game.

13 April 1983

Cheltenham's charge towards the Southern League Midland Division title took a knock when they were beaten 4–1 at fellow challengers Sutton Coldfield Town – their heaviest defeat of the season. Gary Stevens scored the Robins' goal in front of 522 fans at Coles Lane. Cheltenham: Odgen, Ryan, Scarrott, Murphy, Cornes, Paterson, Berry, Stevens, Lewis, Pemberton, Tester.

13 April 1991

Cheltenham took a big step towards Conference safety with a 2–1 win at Telford United, thanks to goals from Paul Brogan and Kevin Willetts. Cheltenham: Barrett, Crouch, Willetts, Brogan, Vircavs, Payne, Bloomfield, Upshall, Camden, Buckland, Jordan.

13 April 1998

A healthy attendance of 3,093 saw Cheltenham lose 2–1 at home to Hereford United. It was their highest gate for a league game since September 2 1968 when 4,069 turned out, also for a match against the Bulls. John Brough scored for Hereford before joining Cheltenham the following summer and helping them progress to the Football League. Cheltenham's only other 3,000+ crowds since 1968 came to see them play Atherstone in April 1973 and Gloucester City in April 1997.

13 April 1999

Neil Grayson's penalty was enough to sink Kingstonian at Whaddon Road. It was the veteran's 21st goal of the season. The game was sandwiched between the two legs of the FA Trophy semi-final between the clubs, which the K's won 5–3 on aggregate. Cheltenham: Book, Duff, Victory, Banks, Freeman, Brough, Howells, Bloomer, Grayson, Bailey, Norton.

14 April 1979

A crowd of 1,415, including many visiting supporters, gathered at Whaddon Road to see Worcester City triumph 2–0 in the Southern League Premier Division. City claimed the championship that season, two years after gaining promotion from Division One North, while Cheltenham's second-half-of-the-season slump saw them fail to qualify for the newly formed Alliance Premier League. Cheltenham: Miles, Caudle, Edwards, Murphy, Foster, Brown, MacKenzie, Fleet, Lewis, Davies, Dangerfield.

14 April 2001

Russell Milton made his 100th start for Cheltenham Town in a 2–1 win over Lincoln City, with defender Michael Duff scoring both goals.

14 April 2007

A 2–0 victory at Oldham Athletic boosted Cheltenham's survival hopes. John Finnigan and Kayode Odejayi were the scorers.

15 April 1960

Two goals in the last five minutes earned Wisbech Town a 3–2 win at Cheltenham before a large Good Friday crowd of 3,231. Clive Burder and Peter Cleland were Cheltenham's scorers. Cheltenham: Gourlay, Farrell, Baird, Geddes, Hyde, Dunn, Carnie, Scott, Cleland, Coldray, Burder.

15 April 1974

Cheltenham consolidated their third place in Southern League Division One (North) with a 3–2 home win over Gloucester City. Pat Casey, Julian Lailey and Dave Lewis found the net and Whaddon Road experienced its first ever streaker! The match was watched by 1,245 fans. Cheltenham: Hall, Thorndale, Lailey, Jones, Jefferies, Griffiths, Cooper, Casey, Lewis, Dangerfield, Bailey. Sub: Casey.

15 April 1995

Lee Howells and Martin Boyle scored in a 2–1 win at Trowbridge Town, keeping Cheltenham Town's Southern League title push going at Frome Road.

16 April 1977

Cheltenham won 8–0 for the second time in a season, brushing Oswestry Town aside on their way to promotion from Division One North of the Southern League.
They had beaten Bedworth United by the same scoreline.
Dave Lewis scored a hat-trick, supplemented by goals from Terry Paterson, Kieron Hehir and Tony Price.

16 April 2001

Chris Banks made his 350th Cheltenham Town start against Blackpool in a 2–2 draw at Bloomfield Road, which was in the process of being rebuilt at the time. Both Robins goals came from Charlton striker Charlie MacDonald, the only strikes of his loan spell.

16 April 2002

Cheltenham Town were held to a goalless draw with Carlisle United, when a win that would have guaranteed them automatic promotion failed to materialise.
A superb goalkeeping display from Peter Keen left 545 travelling fans frustrated at Brunton Park, the pick of his saves as a result of a Michael Duff header.

17 April 1993

Jimmy Smith's goal ended Dover Athletic's twenty-three-month unbeaten home record. The Crabble club still went on to claim the Beazer Homes League title, with Cheltenham finishing second.

17 April 1995

Cheltenham drew 1–1 at home to Gloucester City, with Lee Howells' goal cancelling out David Holmes' opener for the Tigers. The match was watched by 2,691 fans, who saw the Robins' title hopes fade.

17 April 1999

Cheltenham missed out on a second successive visit to Wembley in the FA Trophy, losing 3–1 at home to a Geoff Pitcher-inspired Kingstonian side in their semi-final second leg. It was Steve Cotterill's first defeat in the competition as Cheltenham manager and Cheltenham's first since January 1997. The London club progressed 5–3 on aggregate.

17 April 2004

Cheltenham's 2–0 win over York City effectively consigned the Minstermen to relegation from the Football League.

18 April 1964

Cheltenham Town's 9-match winning run was ended 2–0 by Kings Lynn.

19 April 1937

Holder scored 5 goals in a 7–0 away win over Evesham Town. Hazard and R. Jones were the other scorers.

19 April 1958

Cheltenham won the Southern League Cup for the one and only time in their history, defeating free-scoring Gravesend & Northfleet over two legs. Cheltenham had knocked out rivals Gloucester City 4–0 on aggregate in the first round and cruised past Bath City 7–0 in round two, the third time the prolific Robins had netted 7 goals that season. Hereford and Guildford were also ousted en route to the final. With former Manchester City goalkeeper Bill Gourlay in fine form between the sticks, Cheltenham put themselves in a commanding position with a 2–0 success at Gravesend in the first leg, with scorers Peter Cleland and Jimmy Geddes. First-half goals from Cleland and Danny Fowler put Cheltenham firmly on course and although Thomas pulled one back for the Fleet, Cheltenham prevailed 4–1 on aggregate. A crowd of nearly 5,000 saw Rex Dunlop presented with the cup by president of the club Sir George Dowty. Cheltenham: Gourlay, Farrel, Baird, Dunlop, Hyde, Dunn, Geddes, Fowler, Cleland, Scott, Burder.

19 April 1986

Chris Townsend scored four times in a 5–3 Alliance Premier League win over Nuneaton Borough at Whaddon Road. John Powell was also on target in front of 939 fans.

20 April 1976

Cheltenham's Southern League Division One (North) campaign ended with a 2–1 home defeat by Worcester City, leaving them in a final position of 5th in the table. John Davies scored their goal, his 9th of the campaign.

20 April 2002

Cheltenham were forced to settle for a place in the play-offs after a 2–0 defeat at Plymouth Argyle, who were crowned League Two champions at Home Park before a crowd of 18,517. Jason Bent put the Pilgrims ahead in the 4th minute, beating Steve Book with a low shot from 12 yards. Defender Graham Coughlan scored the second in the 24th minute after Russell Milton's attempted clearance hit John Finnigan and spun back towards goal. The ball squirmed out of Steve Book's grasp and Coughlan smashed the ball in from close range. Cheltenham: Book, Griffin, Brough (Howarth), M. Duff, Victory, Williams (Tyson), Yates, Finnigan, Milton, Alsop (Grayson), Naylor.

21 April 2001

A 3–1 home defeat by Kidderminster Harriers virtually ended any lingering play-off hopes for Cheltenham Town in their second Football League campaign. Neil Grayson scored the Robins' goal.

21 April 2012

A Crewe Alexandra team, unbeaten in 14 games, beat Cheltenham in a play-off dress rehearsal at Gresty Road.

22 April 1967

Joe Gadston scored a hat-trick in a 3–0 home win over Bath City.

22 April 1999

The most dramatic of 3–2 triumphs over Yeovil Town secured the Conference title. Jamie Victory, Neil Grayson and Michael Duff were the scorers, with Duff's 97th-minute winner from Keith Knight's cross the goal that took the club into the Football League, although Victory remains adamant it was his goal. An official crowd of 6,150 crammed into Whaddon Road. Cheltenham: Book, Duff, Banks, Brough, Freeman, Victory, Howells, Bloomer, Norton, Grayson, Bailey (Knight). Subs not used: Yates, Eaton.

23 April 1983

Cheltenham Town beat Aylesbury United 3–0 on their way to the Southern League Midland Division title. The goals came from Duncan Berry, Norman Pemberton and an own goal; 572 turned up to watch.

24 April 1976

Cheltenham beat Gloucester City 2–0 at Horton Road in the Gloucestershire Senior Cup final to regain the trophy. The goals came from Dave Lewis' penalty and a Colin Mousdale own goal. Cheltenham: Miles, Scarrott, Lailey, Davies, Murphy, Collicutt, Skeen, Hall, Lewis, Hehir, Dangerfield.

24 April 1992

Jimmy Smith scored an early scrambled goal but Cheltenham went on to lose 4–2 in the Conference at FA Trophy finalists Witton Albion, a result that virtually consigned the Robins to relegation. Steve Brooks added a second goal near the end, but it was too little, too late. Cheltenham: Nicholls, Howells, Willetts, Clark, Vircavs, Owen, Brooks, J. Smith, Henry, Warren, Buckland.

24 April 1994

Cheltenham played Waterlooville in a Sunday afternoon match, twenty-four hours after drawing 1–1 at Burton Albion. Paul Mortimore's goal for Cheltenham separated the teams. Cheltenham: Thomas, Bloomer, S. Jones, Clark, N. Smith, Cooper, Howells Owen, J. Smith, Mortimore, Warren. Subs: Diaz, Lovell.

25 April 1975

Dave Lewis scored his 53rd goal of the season in a 3–1 defeat at Milton Keynes City.

25 April 1987

Chris Townsend scored his 27th and final goal of the campaign in a 2–0 win over Welling United. He scored 22 in the league and became the first Cheltenham player to score more than 20 goals in a Conference season.

25 April 2000

A strong Aston Villa team played at Cheltenham in a benefit match for Chris Banks. Villa ran out 6–1 winners with goals from Benito Carbone, Lee Hendrie and Dion Dublin. Richard Walker replied for the Robins. Villa fan Banks was given a chance to play for the Claret and Blues in the second half and more than 3,000 fans turned out to show their support and see Villa's stars. Villa had also visited for Dave Lewis' testimonial match in May 1992, when Cheltenham won 4–3.

25 April 1998

Cheltenham drew 1–1 with newly crowned Conference champions Halifax Town in what was a day of double celebration as Robins fans sang: 'Good luck in Division Three, we're going to Wembley' as they looked forward to the FA Trophy final at Wembley.

25 April 2009

Cheltenham drew 1–1 at home against Carlisle United, confirming their relegation to League Two after three seasons in the third tier.

26 April 2003

Michael Duff played up front and shone in a 3–0 home win over Blackpool as Cheltenham kept their survival hopes alive under boss Bobby Gould. Duff scored one, with Tony Naylor bagging a brace.

27 April 1985

Cheltenham were beaten 4–1 at Fisher in the second leg of the Southern League Cup final. They went down 6–2 on aggregate. Paul Collicutt scored the only goal for John Murphy's men.

27 April 2002

Cheltenham drew 1–1 at Hartlepool United in the first leg of their first ever play-off semi-final. Neil Grayson scored a late equaliser to set things up nicely for the second leg at Whaddon Road. Cheltenham had made the long journey north with three senior players – Chris Banks, Lee Howells and Russell Milton – out injured. Boss Steve Cotterill adapted the team to a 4-5-1 formation with Mark Yates playing in front of the back four and both Martin Devaney and Neil Grayson supporting Julian Alsop from wide positions. It worked well, and tellingly, Cotterill chose to stick with the game plan even after Eifion Williams had given Hartlepool a lead on the stroke of half-time. He scored with a well-directed header 8 yards out from a curling cross by right-back Micky Barron. Cheltenham had chances to level before they did – Jamie Victory's shot against the bar being the best of them, but with two minutes to go Grayson – such a wonderful servant to the club – rolled back the years to smash in the equaliser after Martyn Lee had blocked a clearance by Chris Westwood and squared the ball to him. Cheltenham: Book, Griffin, M. Duff, Walker, Victory, Devaney (Williams), Finnigan, Yates, Lee, Grayson, Alsop.

27 April 2004

Left-back Jamie Victory signed a new two-year deal with Cheltenham, which would take him up to a decade of service to the club. He has made more starts in the Football League for the Robins than any other player.

28 April 1984

Goals from Nick Jordan and Nick Gazzard earned Cheltenham Town a 2–2 draw with Sutton Coldfield Town in their final Southern League Premier Division home match of the season. The result helped to consolidate the Robins in a comfortable mid-table position, but consigned their visitors from Birmingham to relegation only a year after going up as Midland Division runners-up to the Robins. Cheltenham: Odgen, Murphy, Scarrott, Collicutt, Cornes, Paterson, Evans, Baverstock, Gazzard, Pemberton, Jordan.

28 April 1990

Cheltenham were well beaten 5–1 by Darlington, who were presented with the Conference shield in front of 5,525 fans. Mickey Nuttell scored the Robins' only goal.

28 April 2007

Cheltenham assured League One survival for the first time, hitting back from 2–0 down to win 4–2 at Rotherham United's old Millmoor Ground. Their goals were scored by Kayode Odejayi, Steve Gillepsie and J.J. Melligan. Cheltenham: Brown, Gill, Townsend, Duff, Armstrong, Melligan, Finnigan, Bird, Caines, Gillespie, Odejayi. Subs not used: Lowe, Connolly, Reid, Yao, Connor.

28 April 2012

Cheltenham Town confirmed their play-off place with a 3–1 home win over Bradford City.

29 April 1933

Cheltenham registered a record league victory, beating Bourneville Athletic 11–0. Haycox and Hazard both scored 4 goals, with Lang, Goodyer and Hill all finding the net.

29 April 1987

Mark Boyland scored in a 2–1 home defeat by Sutton United on the final day of the Conference season. He and Chris Townsend scored 50 of Cheltenham's 93 goals scored that season.

29 April 1989

Mark Buckland and Mark Boyland both scored in a 2–2 home draw with Fisher Athletic in the Conference.

29 April 2000

John Brough's goal sank Chester City 1–0 at Whaddon Road and took Cheltenham to within a whisker of a play-off place at the end of their first season in the Football League.

29 April 2006

A 2–0 home win over Notts County confirmed Cheltenham Town's play-off place under boss John Ward.

30 April 1956

Cheltenham beat Tonbridge 1–0 thanks to Danny Mitchinson's strike, earning them a runners-up finish in the Southern League, which was their highest position achieved in their history.

30 April 1958

Cheltenham finished their season with a 7–1 win over Lovells Athletic, with goals from Fowler, Cleland and Dunlop. Cleland ended the season with 37 goals, Fowler 35 and Dunlop 21. Cheltenham scored 115 goals in 42 games, ending sixth in the Southern League.

30 April 1977

Cheltenham beat Barry Town 3–0, sealing promotion back to the Southern League Premier Division after an absence of eight years. A crowd of 1,772 saw goals from Terry Paterson, Kieron Hehir and John Davies secure the win. Dave Lewis finished the season with 28 goals.

30 April 1980

Cheltenham's season in the Southern League Midland Division limped towards a disappointing conclusion with a home game against Stourbridge. The Robins, who had taken only 1 point from their previous 10 games, fell to a 2–1 defeat in their final home game before a crowd of just 137 – one of the lowest ever for a first team home match. John Davies scored the Cheltenham goal ten minutes from the end. Cheltenham: Taylor, Caudle, Rice, Humphries, Hams, Brinkworth, Dangerfield, Davies, Lewis, Reed, Gardner.

30 April 1985

Mark Boyland scored a hat-trick in a 3–2 win over Gloucester City.

30 April 2002

Cheltenham beat Hartlepool on penalties to reach the play-off final. Paul Arnison put Hartlepool ahead in the 17th minute, but a spectacular strike by Lee Williams levelled the scores nine minutes later, and with the tie locked at 2–2 on aggregate; a shoot-out was necessary. Neil Grayson, Martyn Lee and Mark Yates all scored from 12 yards, but Michael Duff missed. John Finnigan held his nerve as did Julian Alsop, meaning Richie Humphreys had to score to keep his side alive, but his spot kick crashed against the bar, hit goalkeeper Steve Book and a post before finally rebounding to safety. Cheltenham: Book, M. Duff, Victory, Yates, Milton (Lee), Griffin, Walker, Alsop, Naylor (Grayson), Williams (Devaney) Finnigan.

MAY

1 May 1991

Chris Burton scored 4 goals in a 5–0 win over Boston United. Kim Casey claimed the other.

1 May 1999

Cheltenham Town received the Conference trophy after a 0–0 draw with Welling United at Whaddon Road. Neil Grayson was named non-league Player of the Year.

1 May 2004

A 1–1 draw at Carlisle United condemned the Cumbrians to relegation from the Football League, with Kayode Odejayi scoring the goal for John Ward's side.

1 May 2010

Cheltenham were thrashed 5–0 by Steve Cotterill's Notts County, who were crowned champions of League Two at Meadow Lane, while the Robins were still not assured of their safety.

2 May 1969

Cheltenham were beaten 3–1 by Dover Athletic on the final day of the season, condemning them to relegation by 0.02 of a goal.

2 May 1988

Cheltenham finished the Conference season with a 1–1 draw against Sutton United. It was their twentieth draw of the campaign, setting a new club record.

2 May 1992

Cheltenham were relegated from the Conference on the final day of the season despite beating Welling United 3–2 at Whaddon Road with goals from Jimmy Smith, Lee Howells and Kevin Willetts in front of 1,197 fans. They finished 2 points adrift of Slough Town, and their total of 45 points was the highest for a relegated team from the Conference at that time. Long-serving defender Willetts finished the season as top scorer with 12.

2 May 1999

Cheltenham paraded their Conference trophy around the town having clinched promotion to the Football League after a 112-year wait.

2 May 2009

Goalkeeper Will Puddy made his only appearance for Cheltenham Town in a 2–0 defeat at Southend United, taking the total number of players used during the season to 51.

3 May 1997

A 0–0 draw at Burton Albion was enough to earn Cheltenham Town a return to the Conference at the expense of county foes Gloucester City. Richard Dunwell missed a penalty, but it did not matter. Gloucester's 3–1 home defeat by Salisbury meant a point was enough for Cheltenham to clinch second place behind champions Gresley Rovers and return to the top echelon of the non-league game after a five-year absence. Cheltenham: Maloy, Duff, Knight, Banks, Freeman, Victory, Howells, Wright, Dunwell (Boyle), Eaton (Cotterill), Bloomer.

3 May 2003

Cheltenham were relegated from League One at the end of their first season at that level after a 1–0 defeat at Notts County on the final day of the campaign.

3 May 2008

Cheltenham Town's heroic 2–1 home win over Doncaster Rovers was enough to stave off the drop for a second successive season. Steven Gillespie and Paul Connor were the scorers for Keith Downing's side, who were indebted to goalkeeper Shane Higgs for a wonderful display between the posts. Cheltenham: Higgs, Gill, Duff, Keogh, Wright, S Brown (Lindegaard), Bird, Russell (Armstrong), Vincent, Connor, Gillespie. Subs not used: S.P. Brown, Connolly, D'Agostino.

4 May 1985

John Murphy's Cheltenham earned promotion to the Gola League with a 2–1 win over Alvechurch, claiming their biggest honour in fifty years. They had to play 12 games in the last twenty-five days of the season, but goals from Mark Boyland and Mark Hughes sealed the win and the Southern League title in front of 1,999 fans. Paul Collicutt lifted the huge Championship shield, despite having been forced to visit hospital for treatment on an injured collar bone. They finished 2 points ahead of Kings Lynn at the top, with 24 wins from their 38 matches. Chairman Arthur Hayward was unable to watch. He was pacing around Pittville Park when Hughes tucked away the all-important penalty. Cheltenham: Moss, Ball, Cornes, Collicutt, Scarrott, Abbley, Baverstock, Hughes, Boyland, Hacker, Jordan. Subs not used: Goff.

4 May 1999

Cheltenham Town played their final match as a non-league club, beating Gloucester City 3–0 in the Gloucestershire Senior Cup final. Clive Walker signed off with a goal in his last Robins appearance.

5 May 1990

Cheltenham Town rounded off their Conference campaign with a 2–1 win over Kidderminster Harriers, with Richard Crowley and Kevin Willetts scoring. Mark Buckland finished as top scorer for the second season running, netting 19 times in 54 appearances.

5 May 2013

Cheltenham Town were beaten 1–0 by Northhampton Town in the second leg of the play-off semi-finals. The only goal was a stunning strike from Luke Guttridge, taking the Cobblers through to face Bradford City in the final at Wembley, with a 2–0 aggregate victory.

6 May 1995

Cheltenham finished their Southern League campaign with a 2–0 defeat at VS Rugby and were presented with the runners-up cup for the third year in succession.

6 May 1997

Goals from Martin Boyle and Lee Howells earned Cheltenham Town the Gloucestershire Senior Cup at Gloucester City's Meadow Park.

6 May 1999

Cheltenham Town's 2–1 defeat at Southend United on the final day of their first Football League campaign cost them a play-off place. Lee Howells put Cheltenham ahead before it all went wrong. Steve Book, Jamie Victory and Mark Yates started all 46 League matches that season.

6 May 2002

Cheltenham Town claimed play-off glory, beating old non-league foes Rushden & Diamonds 3–1 with goals from Martin Devaney, Julian Alsop and John Finnigan in front of a crowd of 24,368. Devaney's 27th minute opener was immediately cancelled out by Paul Hall's solo effort, but Cheltenham powered home in the second half to climb into the third tier of English football for the first time. It was Steve Cotterill's last match in charge before leaving to take over at Stoke City. Cheltenham: Book, Griffin, Victory, Duff, Walker, Williams, Yates, Finnigan, Devaney (Grayson), Naylor, Alsop. Subs not used: Howarth, Muggleton, Lee, Tyson.

6 May 2006

John Ward made changes to his Robins team with a play-off place already secured and they thumped Mansfield Town 5–0 at Field Mill, with David Bird netting the first goal of his career from the penalty spot. Steven Gillespie, Ashley Vincent, Grant McCann and Kayode Odejayi were the other scorers. Cheltenham: Higgs, Gallinagh, Caines, Duff, Bell, Vincent, Bird, McCann (Connolly), Wilson, Guinan (Odejayi), Gillespie (Spencer). Subs not used: Brown, Wylde.

6 May 2008

Adam Connolly, Craig Reid, Michael Wylde and Sam Foley were all released by Cheltenham Town boss Keith Downing.

7 May 1983

Cheltenham sealed the Southern League Midland Division title with a 0–0 draw against Wellingborough at Whaddon Road. A point was enough to take top spot, with promotion already guaranteed with a 2–0 win over Forest Green Rovers five days earlier.

7 May 2011

Cheltenham drew 1–1 at Stockport County, with Brian Smikle scoring in what was the Edgeley Park club's final match before relegation from the Football League.

8 May 2004

Shane Duff's goal earned Cheltenham Town a 1–1 draw with Huddersfield Town, denying the Yorkshire club automatic promotion. It was the highest attendance of the season, with 5,814 there to see it – 1,793 of those being Terriers fans. Andy Booth scored his 100th goal for Huddersfield, while Cheltenham's Damian Spencer was sent off for two yellow cards. Shane Higgs was named Robins' supporters' Player of the Year.

8 May 2010

Cheltenham Town secured Football League survival with a 1–1 home draw against Accrington Stanley, with Josh Low scoring in the ninth minute to settle the nerves. A crowd of 3,856 assembled at the Abbey Business Stadium.

9 May 2002

Cheltenham manager Steve Cotterill's incredible five-year reign came to an end. Fans said at the time that he should be given the freedom of Cheltenham.

9 May 2002

Neil Grayson, the man who scored Cheltenham Town's first Football League goal, topped the list of six players being released by the Robins. Steve Cotterill had the unenviable task of informing the six – Grayson, Steve Benbow, Gareth Hopkins, Michael Jackson, Hugh McAuley and Jason White – that they would not be offered new deals. In addition, defenders Keith Hill and Steve Jones and goalkeeper Carl Muggleton were placed on the transfer list.

9 May 2011

Ruthless Cheltenham Town boss Mark Yates released five players and placed club captain Michael Pook on the transfer list. Martin Riley, Frankie Artus, J.J. Melligan, Jake Lee and Daniel Lloyd-Weston were all shown the exit door.

9 May 2012

Chairman Paul Baker described the job done by Cheltenham Town boss Mark Yates and his assistant Neil Howarth as 'better than anyone could have expected' after they signed new two-year contracts.

10 May 2001

Cheltenham boss Steve Cotterill told the club's Player of the Year, Mark Yates, to take a well-deserved rest over the summer. While the majority of the squad had been given fitness programmes to follow, Cotterill was concerned that the midfield dynamo did not suffer burn out. So he asked the former Kidderminster star to put his feet up before reporting back for preseason training.

11 May 2004

Steve Guinan joined Cheltenham Town on a two-year deal from Hereford United. He scored 25 goals in 34 starts for the Bulls in the Conference the previous season. John Ward released nine players on the same day: Bob Taylor; Steve Book; Antony Griffin; Richard Forsyth; Paul Brayson; Ben Cleverley; Lee Howells; Craig Dobson; and Luke Buttery. Book and Howells had made 766 starts between them. Jerry Gill and Shane Higgs signed new deals, while Graham Fyfe, John Brough and Luke Corbett were offered contracts. John Finnigan and Jamie Victory had penned two-year contracts already.

12 May 2004

Shane Duff was invited to Torquay United's promotion party, having scored the goal which denied Huddersfield Town a top three place and allowed the Gulls to capitalise. Torquay were promoted thanks to a 2–1 win at Southend United.

13 May 2006

Goals from John Finnigan and Steve Guinan earned Cheltenham Town a 2–1 lead after the first leg of their play-off semi-final at Wycombe Wanderers. Tommy Mooney's late goal restored hope for the Chairboys ahead of the second leg at Whaddon Road. Cheltenham: Higgs, Gill, Duff, Caines, Armstrong, Vincent, Finnigan, McCann, Wilson (Bell), Guinan (Gillespie), Odejayi (Spencer). Subs not used: Bird, Brown.

13 May 2012

Cheltenham Town took a commanding 2–0 lead in their play-off semi-final first leg against Torquay United, with goals from Jermaine McGlashan and Ben Burgess. The crowd was 5,273. Cheltenham: Brown, Lowe, Bennett, Elliott, Jombati, McGlashan, Pack, Summerfield, Mohamed (Smikle), Spencer (Goulding), Burgess (Duffy).

14 May 2002

Cheltenham took an open-top bus tour of the town to celebrate their play-off triumph and first promotion to the Football League.

15 May 2010

Shane Duff's testimonial took place at Whaddon Road, with a Robins Legends XI taking on the first team.

16 May 2003

Cheltenham manager Bobby Gould made his first signing of the summer, landing nineteen-year-old Crystal Palace player Craig Dobson. The right-sided midfielder played in Cheltenham's last four reserve games of the 2002/03 season and impressed with his pace, trickery on the ball and crossing ability. Dobson, from Chingford in Essex, had been with Crystal Palace for three years on their scholarship programme, but was told he would not be offered a professional contract by the Selhurst Park club. He turned down an offer from top Romanian club FC Arges Dacia to join Cheltenham.

17 May 1998

Cheltenham Town claimed their first piece of major silverware, defeating Southport 1–0 at Wembley courtesy of Jason Eaton's 79th-minute header from Russell Milton's free-kick. More than 18,000 fans made the pilgrimage to West London to cheer on their team, swelling the crowd to 26,837. Steve Cotterill was named non-league Manager of the Year for leading the Robins to the Trophy, as well as runners-up spot in the Conference in their first campaign since stepping back up from the Southern League. Cheltenham: Book, Duff, Banks, Freeman, Victory, Knight (Smith), Howells, Bloomer, Eaton, Watkins, Walker (Milton). Sub not used: Wright.

17 May 2012

Cheltenham made their second appearance at Wembley and the first at the newly built stadium after a 2–1 play-off semi-final second leg win at Torquay United in front of a crowd of 3,606. Goalkeeper Scott Brown made a string of outstanding saves, and Jermaine McGlashan and Marlon Pack scored the goals that earned Cheltenham a 4–1 victory on aggregate. Cheltenham: Brown, Lowe, Bennett, Elliott, Jombati, McGlashan (Hooman), Pack, Summerfield, Mohamed, Spencer (Penn), Burgess (Goulding).

18 May 1998

Cheltenham paraded the FA Trophy around town, with 12,000 jubilant fans taking to the streets to toast the club's success.

18 May 2006

Cheltenham held out for a 0–0 draw at home to Wycombe Wanderers to progress to the play-off final for the second time in their history under John Ward's management.

19 May 2008

Lee Ridley and Aaron Ledgister were told they could leave Cheltenham Town. Left-back Ridley was signed from Scunthorpe the previous summer on a three-year contract but an injury and the arrival of Alan Wright kept him on the sidelines after ten first-team games, and he ended the season on loan at Lincoln City. Winger Ledgister made a substitute appearance in the Carling Cup at Southend in August, and had loan spells at Weston-super-Mare and Bath City.

20 May 2006

Tickets for the Coca-Cola League Two play-off final between Cheltenham Town and Grimsby Town at the Millennium Stadium in Cardiff on Sunday, 28 May went on sale. The Robins were allocated the northern end of the stadium.

21 May 2003

Richard Kear, the first Forest footballer to sign professional terms at Cheltenham Town, was released by the Whaddon Road club. Kear, then nineteen, signed professionally after impressing previous boss Steve Cotterill. At the start of the last season he was knocking on the door of the first-team, but the arrival of Bobby Gould as manager saw Kear's star fall from its ascendancy. Ironically, while Kear found his face no longer fitted under Gould, his former Cinderford teammate Dave Bird was catapulted from the youth team set-up into the first team. Within months, Bird was named young Player of the Year at the Robins while Kear was told he would not be getting a new contract.

22 May 2003

Dave Reynolds resigned from the board of Cheltenham Town after eighteen months as director. He had been chairman of Kidderminster Harriers for eighteen years, working alongside manager Graham Allner. On his departure from Cheltenham, Reynolds denied that his decision to leave Whaddon Road was due to Allner's sacking by Cheltenham in February.

22 May 2011

Burton Albion manager Paul Peschisolido spoke of his disappointment at losing club record signing Russ Penn to Cheltenham Town. Penn's contract with the Brewers expired and he turned down the offer of a new deal in order to make the move to Whaddon Road. The twenty-five-year-old was reunited with manager Mark Yates, who sold him to Albion for £20,000 while in charge of Kidderminster Harriers in July 2009. Penn made 89 appearances during his two seasons at the Pirelli Stadium.

23 May 2011

Midfielder pair Marlon Pack and Russ Penn agreed two-year contracts with Cheltenham Town. Pack joined permanently after a successful loan spell, with boss Mark Yates saying he wanted to build a team around the playmaker.

24 May 1947

Cheltenham ended their season with a 4–0 home win over Dartford, with Crowe netting a hat-trick and Peter Goring scoring the other.

25 May 2004

Defender or midfielder Andy Gallinagh, nineteen, accepted a three-month contract with Cheltenham Town. He played for their under-19s the previous season and made a handful of appearances for the reserves.

26 May 2002

Stoke City announced the appointment of Cheltenham Town's manager Steve Cotterill as their new boss. Cotterill, who steered Cheltenham into League One via the play-offs, signed a three-year contract. The thirty-seven-year-old worked alongside director of football John Rudge and first-team coach Dave Kevan. He replaced Gudjon Thordarson, who was sacked four days after taking the Potters into the Championship after a 2–0 play-off final success against Brentford in Cardiff.

27 May 2012

Cheltenham lost in the play-offs for the first time, going down 2–0 to Crewe Alexandra at Wembley Stadium. The Railwaymen's goals came from Nick Powell and Byron Moore. The attendance was 24,029. Cheltenham: Brown, Jombati, Bennett, Elliott, Garbutt, McGlashan, Pack (Penn), Summerfield, Mohamed, Goulding (Duffy), Burgess (Spencer).

28 May 2006

Cheltenham booked their return to League One after a three-season absence, beating Grimsby Town 1–0 at the Millennium Stadium courtesy of Steve Guinan's goal in the 63rd minute. Grant McCann saw a second-half penalty saved by Steve Mildenhall in front of the largest crowd, to date, ever to witness a Robins match (29,196). Shane Higgs made a vital save with ten minutes left, reacting superbly to deny Gary Jones, who had met Junior Mendes' cross from the right with a firm header. Cheltenham: Higgs, Gill, Caines, Duff, Armstrong (Bell), Vincent (Spencer), Finnigan, McCann, Wilson, Guinan, Gillespie (Odejayi). Subs not used: Brown, Bird.

29 May 2002

Cheltenham Town named Graham Allner as their new manager. Allner – the club's reserve team boss – replaced Steve Cotterill, who signed a three-year contract with First Division Stoke City. Allner was the unanimous choice of the Robins board, who felt it was important to build on the success of the previous five years by selecting someone who was well-liked and respected by the players. Allner had had a successful spell as manager of Kidderminster Harriers and joined the Robins' coaching staff three years earlier. Mike Davis continued in his role as assistant manager to Allner.

29 May 2003

Bobby Gould finally got his man, but Kayode Odejayi's long anticipated switch from Forest Green to Cheltenham Town was destined for the courts. The towering Nigerian-born marksman agreed terms that secured his dream of a return to the Football League, after ten months in the Conference. But Cheltenham failed to agree a fee for the twenty-one-year-old's transfer with Rovers, forcing the matter to an FA Tribunal under the Bosman ruling.

29 May 2006

Thousands of fans lined the streets to give promoted Cheltenham Town a triumphant homecoming. The heroes held the silver trophy aloft to a sea of cheering fans as they toured Cheltenham in an open-top red Stagecoach bus decorated with banners.

30 May 2002

Graham Allner admitted that he thought the chance of being a Football League manager had passed him by. The experienced Allner was officially unveiled as Steve Cotterill's successor at Cheltenham Town.

30 May 2012

Mark Yates said he would hold talks with loan striker Ben Burgess over the possibility of a permanent move to Cheltenham Town. The thirty-year-old target man finished the season on loan to the Robins from Notts County, scoring 3 goals in 9 starts, including a header in the first leg of the play-off semi-final win over Torquay. Yates also hinted that he would like to bring young Huddersfield forward Jimmy Spencer back to the club next season after a successful long-term loan stint during the 2011/12 campaign.

31 May 2007

Striker Kayode Odejayi joined Barnsley for a club record fee of £200,000, turning down a new deal at Whaddon Road.

JUNE

1 June 2001

Carl Muggleton signed for Cheltenham Town on a two-year deal after his release from Stoke City a fortnight earlier.

1 June 2006

Talks broke down between boss John Ward and striker Steve Guinan over a new deal, but the play-off-final hero eventually agreed a one-year contract.

1 June 2010

Ex-Robins boss John Ward was named manager of Colchester United.

1 June 2011

Wesley Thomas joined Crawley Town on a two-year deal after turning down the offer of a new contract at Cheltenham Town. He scored 19 goals for the Robins,who signed him from Dagenham & Redbridge.

1 June 2012

Big striker Ben Burgess signed for Tranmere Rovers after a successful loan spell with Cheltenham Town at the end of the 2011/12 campaign, but the target man soon announced his retirement and began a new career as a teacher.

2 June 2009

Martin Allen announced he would undertake a sponsored bike ride from his Maidenhead home to Whaddon Road to raise funds for his playing budget.

3 June 2010

Award-winning groundsman Matt Rainey joined Cheltenham Town from Forest Green Rovers.

4 June 2001

Robins defender Mark Freeman joined Conference side Boston United for £15,000. The thirty-one-year-old centre-half agreed a three-year contract with the Lincolnshire club, who had just turned full-time. Freeman moved to the Robins from Gloucester City for £7,500 in March 1996 and played 224 games during his spell at Whaddon Road . 'It's been the most difficult outgoing transfer I've had to deal with and I'm very sad he's leaving,' manager Steve Cotterill said. 'I've had a great relationship with Boka over the years. He's got himself a three-year contract which gives him and his family a lot more security.' Cotterill filled the gap left by Freeman's departure by recruiting Keith Hill on a free transfer from Rochdale.

4 June 2003

Former Wales assistant manager Graham Williams became Cheltenham Town manager Bobby Gould's chief scout. Williams was number two to Gould during the latter's reign as manager of the Welsh national side between August 1995 and June 1999.

4 June 2007

Craig Armstrong left Cheltenham Town for Gillingham and it was also announced J.J. Melligan was set to join Leyton Orient. Armstrong, thirty-two, signed a two-year contract with Gillingham, while Melligan was expected to seal a three-year deal with Orient. Both players turned down improved terms from Cheltenham before deciding to move on, and were expected to nearly double their wages. Armstrong estimated he had spent nearly £20,000 on living expenses and travelling from his home in Nottingham while playing for Cheltenham, and he said the Gillingham offer was too good to turn down.

5 June 2007

Cheltenham Town's proposed groundshare agreement with League One rivals Bristol Rovers would be worth 'a substantial six-figure sum' to the club, said chairman Paul Baker. Rovers were due to move to Cheltenham Whaddon Road from the middle of the 2007/08 campaign until the end of 2008/09, but plans for the redevelopment of their Memorial Stadium fell through and the groundshare did not happen.

5 June 2012

Chairman Paul Baker said that the investors who pumped £500,000 into Cheltenham Town's coffers the previous summer wished to remain nameless. Shortly before the start of the 2011/12 campaign, the Robins' board was given extra funds, helping to finance the 'bonus' signings of Luke Summerfield and Darryl Duffy. Both players became key figures in the Robins' League Two promotion bid, which saw them reach the play-off final before going down 2–0 against Crewe Alexandra at Wembley. Baker said the financial assistance had been granted for all the right reasons, with no intention of gaining publicity.

6 June 1979

Cheltenham Town signed John Williams from Abergavenny.

7 June 2009

Striker Ryan Lowe became the second player to snub Cheltenham Town and sign for a League Two rival. The thirty-year-old former Chester City forward agreed a two-year deal to join promotion favourites Bury, despite receiving an offer from the Robins.

8 June 2007

Swansea City midfielder Kristian O'Leary emerged as a transfer target for Cheltenham Town. The twenty-nine-year-old made a big impression at Whaddon Road during his five-game loan spell during the 2006/07 campaign, scoring one goal. He was out of contract at Swansea.

9 June 2004

Mark Yates was linked with a coaching job at Burnley under his old Cheltenham Town boss, Steve Cotterill.

10 June 2003

Defender Neil Howarth joined Conference club
Telford United after his release from Cheltenham Town.

10 June 2010

Port Vale manager Micky Adams boosted his attacking
options by capturing former Cheltenham Town striker
Justin Richards on a two-year deal.

10 June 2011

Mark Yates admitted some of the wages being offered
to players by other League Two clubs had reached
'ridiculous' levels. The Cheltenham Town boss was
working hard to improve his squad, aiming to bring
in five more new faces, with two strikers, a winger,
a centre-half and a goalkeeper on his shopping list.
He confirmed he was not looking for a new left-back as
cover for Danny Andrew.

11 June 2003

Striker Julian Alsop held talks with Cheltenham Town's League Two rivals Oxford United. Alsop, leading scorer for the past two seasons, was told by boss Bobby Gould that he could leave at the end of the season.

12 June 2012

Central defender Steve Elliott signed a one-year contract extension with Cheltenham.

13 June 2005

John Brough agreed terms with Aldershot Town after being released by Cheltenham Town. Brough joined the Conference club on a two-year deal, with the second year conditional on playing in a certain percentage of games in the first.

14 June 2010

Manager Mark Yates hoped Scott Brown and Andy Gallinagh would trigger a clutch of out-of-contract players re-signing for Cheltenham Town. Goalkeeper Brown and the versatile Gallinagh agreed fresh two-year contracts. Yates was waiting to hear back from Shane Duff, Michael Pook, David Bird and Josh Low.

15 June 1974

Denis Allen was appointed Cheltenham's player-manager.

16 June 2009

A squad of Robins fans that would take on Cheltenham Town's Legends of 1999 XI was announced. Each player pledged £60 for the right to face the heroes of Cheltenham's Nationwide Conference title success at the Abbey Business Stadium on Sunday, 12 July 2009. Money raised from the event was donated to Kidney Research UK, with the Robins Trust also claiming a third of the proceeds. The Legends team was managed by Steve Cotterill, who guided the Robins from the Southern League to the third level of English football between 1997 and 2002.

17 June 2008

Alex Russell urged Cheltenham Town to aim high after signing a two-year contract at Whaddon Road. The thirty-five-year-old midfielder became boss Keith Downing's first new recruit of the summer. He spent the second half of the 2007/08 season on loan at Cheltenham from Bristol City and was released by the Championship club at the end of the campaign. Russell made 12 starts and one substitute appearance during his four-month temporary spell, scoring twice. His second-half strike against Leeds United, to put the Robins 2–0 up at Elland Road, was one of the goals of the season. A talented ball player, Russell's vision and set piece skills helped to turn Cheltenham's season around and put them on the road to eventual safety.

17 June 2013

Veteran striker Jamie Cureton joined Cheltenham Town on a one-year deal after leaving Exeter City.

18 June 2008

Craig Armstrong agreed a new one-year contract with Cheltenham Town. The versatile thirty-three-year-old became the fourth player to sign an extended deal with the Robins since the end of the previous campaign.

19 June 2007

Scunthorpe United left-back Lee Ridley emerged as a transfer target for Cheltenham Town. Ridley, who still had a year left to run on his contract at Glanford Park, was told he could leave the League One champions in search of regular first-team football. League Two trio Lincoln City, Bradford City and Rochdale were also believed to be interested in signing the twenty-five-year-old. Cheltenham were short of options on the left following the release of full-backs Jamie Victory and Mickey Bell, coupled with the loss of utility man Craig Armstrong to Gillingham on a free transfer.

20 June 2011

Kaid Mohamed signed a two-year contract with Cheltenham Town.

21 June 2002

Midfielder Hugh McAuley agreed to return to Graham Allner's Cheltenham Town after being released by former manager Steve Cotterill at the end of the previous season.

22 June 2010

Danny Andrew signed a two-year contract with Cheltenham Town having impressed during a loan spell from Peterborough United during the 2009/10 campaign.

23 June 2004

Graham Fyfe agreed another one-year contract with Cheltenham Town manager John Ward.

24 June 2002

Ian Weston left Forest Green Rovers to become Cheltenham Town's new senior sports therapist, nine years after he left Whaddon Road with a broken ankle. Bristol-based Weston, thirty-four, was on loan for two months to the Robins in 1993, while Lindsay Parsons was manager, but it was cut short when he sustained the injury. Weston took over from Andy Mitchell, who was the club's first and only previous full-time physiotherapist.

25 June 1957

Clive Walker was born in Oxford. He signed for Cheltenham Town forty years later, helping them win the FA Trophy and Conference title between 1997 and 1999.

25 June 2010

Josh Low said his enjoyment of the previous season persuaded him to extend his career as a full-time footballer. The thirty-one-year-old turned down the offer of a job as a solicitor to pen a two-year deal with Cheltenham Town. After a hugely frustrating first season at the club, Low started to demonstrate his quality last term, performing well on the wing, and at full-back when called upon. He made 42 appearances, compared with 15 during the 2008/09 campaign.

26 June 2001

Former England international Tony Cottee turned down a move to Cheltenham Town. Robins boss Steve Cotterill had hoped to lure the thirty-five-year-old to Whaddon Road to spearhead his strikeforce.

27 June 2010

Cheltenham Town boss Mark Yates confirmed he was mulling over an approach for ex-Robins winger J.J. Melligan. The skilful twenty-eight-year-old was with Dundalk in the League of Ireland Premier Division having left Leyton Orient.

28 June 2010

Cheltenham Town boss Mark Yates was aiming for another two new faces after capturing defender Keith Lowe's signature. The addition of former loan player Lowe, along with the signing of four youth team graduates, took the Robins squad to 15 professionals.

29 June 2006

John Ward signed a new five-year contract with Cheltenham Town, having guided the club back into the third tier in his second full season at the helm.

30 June 1974

Midfielder Ken Skeen signed for Cheltenham Town. The ex-Swindon Town and Oxford United man can still be found in the press box at home games working for the Press Association. Ex-Reading man Tony Wagstaffe also arrived at the club.

JULY

1 July 2003

Bobby Gould took his Cheltenham Town squad to the racecourse for a preseason running session. The squad were joined by eight trialists, including Graham Fyfe, Bertrand Cozic and Ben Cleverley, who all earned contracts. Gould joined in with some of the running himself, but ruled out signing League Two forms!

1 July 2010

Wesley Thomas and Frankie Artus joined Cheltenham Town, while midfielder Michael Pook was named club captain by boss Mark Yates.

2 July 2007

Striker Martin Paterson was shown around the Seasons training ground and almost joined Cheltenham, but the move failed to materialise.

3 July 1997

Russell Milton joined Cheltenham from Dover Athletic for a bargain fee of around £4,000.

3 July 2007

Left-back Lee Ridley signed on a three-year contract from Scunthorpe United.

4 July 2011

Republic of Ireland international Alan Bennett joined Cheltenham Town following his release from Wycombe Wanderers on a one-year deal, with the option of a second season.

5 July 2011

Portuguese full-back Sido Jombati joined Cheltenham Town on a one-year contract, having been recommended to Mark Yates by his former teammate and Bath City assistant manager Lee Howells.

6 July 2004

Michael Duff joined Steve Cotterill's Burnley for a fee of £30,000, plus a friendly match between the clubs at Whaddon Road. Duff has played at all levels, from the Hellenic League Premier Division to the Premier League, in a remarkable career.

7 July 2004

Attacking midfielder and Ireland Under-21 international J.J. Melligan joined Cheltenham Town on a three-year deal from Wolves, costing the club £25,000.

8 July 2003

Cheltenham Town boss Bobby Gould confirmed his interest in striker Bob Taylor and defender Andy Legg. Former Gillingham striker Robert Taylor was also due to train with Cheltenham Town. The powerful thirty-two-year-old was looking for a club after being hit by injuries for the past two seasons.

8 July 2008

Summer signing Alex Russell was on target as Cheltenham Town opened their preseason programme with a comfortable victory over non-league Didcot Town. New recruit from Bristol City, Russell, who enjoyed a successful loan spell at Whaddon Road the previous season, demonstrated how important a player he could become for the Robins when he curled in the opening goal in the 9th minute at the NPower Loop Meadow Stadium. Trialist Michael Husbands was brought down by Martin Brown, and Russell stepped up to dispatch the resulting free-kick past goalkeeper Michael Watkins from 25 yards.

9 July 2004

Former Cheltenham Town defender Antony Griffin was signed for Dorchester Town. The right-back, who became Cheltenham's then joint-record signing when he joined for £25,000 from AFC Bournemouth in 1999, was offered a two-year contract at the Conference South club. He was one of nine players not offered new contracts by Cheltenham manager John Ward at the end of the 2003/04 season.

9 July 2011

Ex-Forest Green goalkeeper Ryan Robinson played forty-five minutes for Cheltenham Town in their opening friendly of the summer at Cirencester Town, but the twenty-eight-year-old free agent was not offered a deal by Mark Yates.

10 July 1997

Goalkeeper Steve Book joined Cheltenham Town from Forest Green Rovers for £8,000 and went on to help the club win two promotions and the FA Trophy at Wembley.

10 July 2008

Gary Hooper turned down a move to Cheltenham Town, signing instead for Scunthorpe United. Keith Downing also missed out on Michael Boulding and Marc Richards before signing Lloyd Owusu.

11 July 2009

Julian Alsop scored for Cheltenham in a friendly match at Weston-super-Mare, pressing his claims for a surprise return to the Robins squad after a spell in non-league football.

12 July 2004

New assistant manager Keith Downing declared himself impressed with the Cheltenham Town set-up. He had just completed his first full week, and the thirty-eight-year-old former Notts County, Wolverhampton Wanderers and Hereford United midfielder said: 'You look at the club and you have to be quietly impressed. It's very well organised. Everyone's attitude has been brilliant. My decision to come here was 70 or 80 per cent John Ward, and the other 20 per cent was seeing the facilities. I've always been impressed with everything John does. I worked with him for a couple of years at Wolves and he knows how I think.' Downing was the reserve team manager at Wolverhampton and left to join Cheltenham earlier in July.

13 July 2009

Barry Hayles agreed a one-year deal with the Robins and immediately set his sights on firing the club straight back into League One. Chairman Paul Baker pulled out all the stops to capture the former Fulham and Bristol Rovers hitman, who was released by Leicester City at the end of the previous season. London-based Hayles was attracting the interest of a number of other clubs, with Luton Town and Stevenage Borough thought to be in the race to sign him, but he had his heart set on a return to Cheltenham, where he had enjoyed two separate loan spells during the 2008/09 campaign.

July 14 2004

Cheltenham Town played a friendly at Bishop's Cleeve, with Gavin Caines and Graham Ward included on trial.

15 July 2002

Steve Cotterill cut the ribbon to officially open a bar named in his honour. More than 100 locals and Robins fans flocked to the Devon Avenue pub, formerly the Golden Miller, to see the ex-Cheltenham Town boss in action. The order of the day was Cotterill's Cocktail – a mix of champagne, vodka and Red Bull. Landlords Richard Benson and Hugh Blair reopened the pub after a £50,000 refit. One half was a dedicated sports bar plastered with photographs of the Robins' most successful boss. The walls were painted red and the entrance hall was red and white stripes – the same as the Cheltenham Town kit. Cotterill, manager of Stoke City at the time, said it was odd seeing his name above the door. 'I was out running and I came past and felt quite strange, but it was a nice feeling,' he said. 'It's touching. I know I must have touched the hearts of people in Cheltenham. I'm very proud of it.' Cotterill guided Cheltenham Town to the team's greatest success – promotion to League One.

15 July 2003

Former Cheltenham Town defender Gary Wotton joined Cirencester Town.

16 July 2010

Steve Elliott signed a two-year deal with Cheltenham Town following his release from Bristol Rovers.

17 July 2003

Russell Milton signed for Bath City after being released by Cheltenham Town, while mercurial thirty-six-year-old Tony Naylor announced he would be leaving the club after negotiations with Bobby Gould over a new deal broke down.

18 July 2002

Cheltenham Town and Forest Green brushed off the summer cobwebs at The Lawn, with former Bristol City marksman Damian Spencer shining in a 4–1 victory on his first appearance in a Robins shirt. Cheltenham boss Graham Allner named all but two of the team that won promotion to League One in the Millennium Stadium play-off final in his first game in charge after taking over from Steve Cotterill. His only changes were to bring in Chris Banks and Hugh McAuley for Richard Walker and the injured Julian Alsop. For Forest Green, there were starts for three of Nigel Spink's summer signings – Alan McLoughlin, Lee Russell and former Cheltenham striker Neil Grayson.

19 July 1997

Cheltenham beat a Wimbledon XI 3–2 at Whaddon Road in a preseason friendly ahead of their return to the Conference under Steve Cotterill. Mark Crisp, Lee Howells and Jimmy Smith scored the goals.

19 July 2001

Cheltenham won 3–0 in a friendly at Evesham United's Common Road, with Hugh McAuley (2) and Russell Milton scoring. Ex-Robins midfielder Giuseppe Licata was in the Evesham side. New arrivals Steve Jones and Keith Hill both featured for Cheltenham.

20 July 2012

Chairman Paul Baker described Cheltenham Town boss Mark Yates as firmly on course to become one of the club's all-time greats. Yates guided the Robins to the League Two play-off final at Wembley in 2012 after a memorable FA Cup run which ended at Tottenham's White Hart Lane earlier in the campaign. Already a legendary player and former captain, Baker praised Yates for his influence in turning Cheltenham around after inheriting a club that was on its knees in December 2009.

21 July 2001

Cheltenham Town drew 0–0 with Huddersfield Town in a preseason friendly at Whaddon Road, watched by a crowd of 1,107. Experienced goalkeeper Carl Muggleton wore a Cheltenham shirt for the first time.

21 July 2011

Former Rangers, Hull City and Swansea City striker Darryl Duffy joined Cheltenham Town on a two-year deal from Bristol Rovers.

22 July 2011

Jimmy Spencer joined Cheltenham Town on a season-long loan deal from Huddersfield Town.

23 July 2003

Cheltenham Town striker Damian Spencer was taken to hospital after a friendly win at Aberystwyth. He injured his ribs when he scored the first goal of the match against the Welsh Premier League side in the 16th minute. He collided with Aberystwyth goalkeeper Jon Worsnop and suffered a heavy fall when heading the ball into the net. He was replaced ten minutes after the goal with Martin Devaney and taken to hospital for a precautionary X-ray.

24 July 2011

Bagasan Graham signed a one-year contract with Cheltenham Town after a successful trial. The eighteen-year-old left-winger, released by Queen's Park Rangers, became manager Mark Yates' ninth new signing of the summer for the Robins.

25 July 1998

John Brough made his first Cheltenham Town appearance in a friendly at Witney Town, scoring twice in a 5–0 victory.

26 July 1979

Cheltenham signed Peter Higgins from Bath City.

27 July 2001

Cheltenham beat Birmingham City 3–1 in a friendly match at Whaddon Road, with Mark Yates, Martin Devaney and Gareth Hopkins the scorers in front of 1,426 fans. Stan Lazaridis replied for the Blues. Cheltenham: Muggleton (Higgs), Howarth (Griffin), M. Duff, Banks, Hill (Victory), Hopkins (Grayson), Yates, McAuley, Howells (Milton), Devaney (White), Alsop. Jerry Gill was in the Blues line-up.

28 July 2004

Former Blackburn Rovers central defender Michael Taylor joined Cheltenham Town.

28 July 2007

Cheltenham were forced to play a preseason friendly against Wolves at Kidderminster Harriers due to the floods affecting the water supply and power at Whaddon Road. Andy Lindegaard scored for the Robins, but Wolves ran out 3–1 winners.

29 July 1983

Cheltenham played a friendly against Shrewsbury Town as part of the Paul Tester transfer deal. Steve Cotterill scored in a 4–1 defeat for the Robins. Tester had joined the Shrews for £10,000 two months earlier.

30 July 2000

Cheltenham played Smiths Athletic at Newlands to make the 60th anniversary of the Smiths club. Julian Alsop scored 4 goals, with Michael Jackson curling in the other, with Robins fan Phil Church making an appearance between the posts for Steve Cotterill's side.

30 July 2006

A Legends XI took on Cheltenham Town to mark Jamie Victory's decade with the Robins.

31 July 1989

Cheltenham were beaten 5–1 at home by a strong Sheffield Wednesday side in a preseason friendly at Whaddon Road. Mark Boyland scored Cheltenham's goal from the penalty spot. Craig Shakespeare scored two of the Owls' goals.

31 July 2001

Jason White scored twice for Cheltenham in a 2–1 win at SVG Einbeck on their preseason tour of Germany.

AUGUST

1 August 2003

It was announced that West Bromwich Albion goal king Bob Taylor was to train with Cheltenham Town the following week. Taylor had been a target for Cheltenham boss Bobby Gould since he learned before the end of the previous season that he would be on the move. The thirty-six-year-old had scored 193 Football League goals from 442 starts and was a big favourite with the Hawthorns fans. He had minor surgery to a knee a month earlier but was declared fit by West Brom's physio.

1 August 2005

Cheltenham Town boss John Ward gave up hope of signing striker James Quinn as he strove to boost his attacking options before the new season. Ward made an offer to ex-Sheffield Wednesday forward Quinn, who was being chased by other clubs, but the Northern Ireland international eventually joined Peterborough United.

1 August 2006

Cheltenham Town Reserves suffered an extra-time defeat in the Pontins Holidays Combination Cup final at Layer Road. Steve Opoka hit the winner for Colchester after Robins striker Michael Whittington had cancelled out the opener from Jamie Guy. Colchester were reduced to ten men midway through the second half when George Elokobi was dismissed for a tackle on Sosthene Yao, but Cheltenham could not take advantage.

1 August 2008

Keith Downing stated that altering players' image of Cheltenham Town as a 'little club' was proving to be his toughest task. The Robins boss was left scratching his head as Marc Richards rejected a £100,000 move to Whaddon Road in favour of remaining with Coca-Cola League Two club Port Vale. Richards became the latest striker Downing had unsuccessfully attempted to sign that summer, following Gary Hooper, Michael and Rory Boulding and Kevin Gall. With a week to go until the new season, Cheltenham had not found a replacement for Steven Gillespie, who joined Colchester United for more than £400,000. Paul Connor and Ashley Vincent were the only fit strikers in the senior squad, with Damian Spencer sidelined by a knee injury.

2 August 1988

Peter Shearer scored on his debut in a 2–2 draw with Kettering Town in the Midland Floodlit Cup.

2 August 1997

Dale Watkins scored the winner in a 1–0 preseason victory over Cardiff City.

2 August 2010

Striker Shaun Jeffers played for England Under-19s against Slovakia at Crewe Alexandra, on loan from Coventry City.

3 August 2005

Sosthene Yao impressed as Cheltenham Town's fledglings hit Cinderford Town for six at the Causeway. Ivory Coast-born Yao, seventeen, teased and tormented the Cinderford defence and deserved more reward than the 85th-minute penalty he scored. Midfielders Scott Musgrove – who joined Cheltenham after being released by Stoke City – and Sam Foley also caught the eye in a Cheltenham team in which right-back Andy Gallinagh, twenty, was the oldest player. Front pair Ashley Vincent and Michael Whittington scored 2 goals each, while Cinderford got a tough workout before the Southern League Division One (West) campaign started. The final score was 6–1 to Cheltenham.

3 August 2006

Steven Gillespie returned to a place in Cheltenham Town's team at Swansea City on the opening day of the season. The striker had been struggling with tightness in his thighs and missed the Robins' final friendly match at Hereford United.

3 August 2007

Cheltenham Town boss John Ward said he had landed an exciting talent after agreeing a one-month loan deal for Bristol City winger Jennison Myrie-Williams. Myrie-Williams, nineteen, broke into Gary Johnson's side the previous season and made 19 starts as City won promotion to the Championship.

4 August 2009

It was announced that Cheltenham Town's new captain Shane Duff would be rewarded for a decade of service with a testimonial year. Duff played for Cheltenham's youth team during the 1999/2000 season before turning professional in October 2000 after a three-month unpaid trial with the senior squad. He made his debut as a substitute against Crewe Alexandra in a 4–0 defeat on Boxing Day in 2002. Duff signed a new one-year contract in the summer of 2009 and was named as John Finnigan's successor as skipper after impressing manager Martin Allen with his leadership skills at a five-day visit to Blandford Army Camp.

4 August 2012

Cheltenham Town were beaten 4–0 in a preseason friendly against Burnley, who included ex-Robins defender Michael Duff in their squad.

5 August 2006

Cheltenham shocked Swansea City 2–1 at the Liberty Stadium on their first match back in League One. The goals came from Grant McCann and Kayode Odejayi, with over 15,000 there to see it.Cheltenham: Higgs, Gill, Caines, Duff (Wilson), Victory, Melligan, Finnigan, McCann, Armstrong, Guinan (Gillespie), Odejayi (Vincent). Subs not used: Bird, Brown.

6 August 2005

Craig Armstrong's debut goal helped Cheltenham to a 2–1 home victory over Bury, with Kayode Odejayi the other scorer in front of 2,967 fans.

7 August 1984

Mark Boyland and Nick Gazzard both scored hat-tricks in a 7–4 win over Sharpness, for whom Kevin Willetts scored twice.

7 August 1999

Cheltenham's first match in the Football League ended in an anticlimax as they went down 2–0 at home to Rochdale. They were the ninth club to make the step up from non-league football. A crowd of 5,189 gathered to witness the historic match.

7 August 2004

Debutant J.J. Melligan was on target along with Kayode Odejayi in a 2–0 win at Southend United, the club's first opening day victory since 1996.

8 August 2006

Kayode Odejayi scored the winner at home to Tranmere Rovers to make it two wins from two games for League Two new boys Cheltenham Town.

9 August 1994

Kevin Willetts' testimonial match was played at Gloucester City against an Aston Villa XI, who won 4–1 at Meadow Park.

9 August 2003

Cheltenham went down 2–0 at Southend United to make it seven years without an opening day success.

10 August 1999

Cheltenham took part in their first ever League Cup tie, going down 2–0 at Norwich City.

10 August 2002

Cheltenham played their first match at League One level, losing 2–0 at home to Wigan Athletic, who went on to win the title that year.

11 August 2007

Steve Gillespie scored the only goal in an opening day win over Gillingham but the striker was sent off.

11 August 2011

Cheltenham Town's home match against Swindon Town was called off due to the riots in Gloucester, but was played twenty-four hours later than planned, with Steve Elliott netting the winner.

12 August 2008

Cheltenham defeated Southend 1–0 at Roots Hall after extra time in the first round of the League Cup, with Ben Gill netting the only goal of the game.

13 August 1998

David Norton signed a one-year contract with
Cheltenham Town after a successful trial following his
departure from Hereford United. He only stayed for
one season, but he made a major impact, helping the
club win promotion back to the Football League and
banishing the painful memories of when he suffered
the drop to the Conference with Hereford in 1997.

13 August 2002

Tony Naylor netted Cheltenham's first ever goal at
League One level, in a 1–1 draw at Barnsley.

14 August 1999

Neil Grayson's booming header from Antony Griffin's
cross earned Cheltenham Town their first ever Football
League win at Mansfield Town's Field Mill. Cheltenham:
Book, Howarth, Banks, Freeman, Victory, Griffin, Yates,
Howells, Devaney (Bloomer), McAuley (Watkins),
Grayson. Subs not used: Duff, Brough, Higgs.

14 August 2001

Steve Cotterill tried – unsuccessfully – to sign Chris
Shuker on loan from Manchester City.

15 August 1970

Dave Lewis made his Cheltenham Town debut in a 3–3 draw at Folkestone.

15 August 1998

Cheltenham's second season back in the Conference started with a 2–1 defeat at Welling United, with Chris Banks scoring the Robins' goal – his 13th for the club and his only strike of the season.

15 August 2001

Barr Construction completed the roof on the new Wymans Road stand at Whaddon Road.

16 August 1997

Cheltenham's first match back in the Conference ended in a 3–0 defeat at Dover Athletic. Steve Book, Russell Milton, Mark Crisp and Dale Watkins all made their debuts at the Crabble Athletic Ground.

16 August 2001

Tony Naylor signed for Cheltenham Town on a two-year deal, finally ending Steve Cotterill's hunt for a proven goalscorer to boost his side's promotion push.

17 August 1974

Denis Allen scored the winner against Bedworth on the opening day of the season in his first match as player/boss.

17 August 1991

Cheltenham lost 1–0 to Witton Albion on the opening day of the 1991/92 season. A poor year saw them relegated to the Southern League after seven years in the Conference.

17 August 1996

Left-back Jamie Victory made his Cheltenham Town debut in a 2–0 home win over Sittingbourne, with goals from Paul Chenoweth and Martin Boyle. Former West Ham and Bournemouth player Victory spent a decade at the club, playing a major part in four promotions.

18 August 1967

Cheltenham Town signed goalkeeper Alan Jefferies from Brentford, a 6ft 3in nineteen-year-old.

18 August 1984

Brian Hughes made his Cheltenham Town debut at home against Gravesend & Northfleet, which ended in a 1–1 draw in front of 437 people. He went on to play 145 consecutive matches before illness in December 1986.

18 August 2001

Tony Naylor made his Cheltenham Town debut as a substitute at Luton Town.

19 August 1997

Goals from Jason Eaton and Jamie Victory earned Cheltenham their first win back in the Conference against Hayes.

19 August 2000

Neil Grayson scored both goals and broke his ankle in a 2–0 win at his hometown club York City. Mark Sertori and Alan Fettis were both in the Minstermen team that day.

20 August 1983

The tenacious Ray Baverstock made his Cheltenham Town debut against Sutton Coldfield Town.

20 August 1994

Chris Banks made his Cheltenham Town debut in a 2–0 win at Rushden & Diamonds. Jimmy Wring and Jason Eaton were the scorers.

21 August 1977

Cheltenham Town lost 2–1 at home to Kuwait, managed by Mario Zagalo, in a friendly match. Kuwait were on a European tour before starting their World Cup qualifying campaign. Their goal came from Colin Hall.

21 August 1993

Former Wales international goalkeeper Martin Thomas made his Cheltenham Town debut in a 5–0 home win over Chelmsford City.

21 August 1999

Hugh McAuley's penalty was enough to earn Cheltenham Town their first home win in the Football League, against Hull City.

21 August 2010

Cheltenham were beaten 6–4 at Rotherham United, for whom Adam Le Fondre scored four times at the Don Valley Stadium.

22 August 1970

Dave Lewis scored the first of his 290 goals for Cheltenham Town in a 2–2 draw at Tonbridge.

22 August 1992

Bob Bloomer made his Robins debut against Chelmsford City, having arrived from Bristol Rovers. The game ended 1–1, with Jimmy Wring on target.

22 August 2000

Cheltenham were unlucky not to win the first leg of their League Cup first-round match at Watford, drawing 0–0 at Vicarage Road.

22 August 2006

Cheltenham knocked Bristol City out of the League Cup with a 2–1 victory at Whaddon Road.

22 August 2009

Cheltenham went down 5–4 in an extraordinary match at home to Bradford City. Elvis Hammond, Michael Townsend and Justin Richards, who netted 2 goals, were the Robins' scorers at Whaddon Road in front of 3,073 fans. Townsend also scored an own goal.

23 August 1997

Cheltenham beat Woking 3–2 at Whaddon Road in the Conference with goals from Jamie Victory, Dale Watkins from the spot and Jason Eaton.

23 August 2003

Damian Spencer scored the first of his two Football League hat-tricks for Cheltenham Town in a 3–3 draw at Hull City's new KC Stadium.

23 August 2005

Cheltenham beat Martin Allen's Brentford 5–0 at home in the first round of the League Cup, thanks to goals from J.J. Melligan, Gavin Caines, Jamie Victory and Grant McCann.

24 August 1985

Cheltenham played their first ever match at Conference level, beating Maidstone 2–1 with goals from Steve Brooks and Brian Hughes. A crowd of 1,082 saw it.

24 August 1999

Cheltenham beat Norwich City 2–1 at Whaddon Road in the second leg of their first ever League Cup tie, but were knocked out 3–2 on aggregate. Neil Grayson put the Robins ahead from the penalty spot in the 47th minute and Jamie Victory took the tie to extra time with a 70th-minute header. Sadly, Lee Marshall's 100th-minute goal was enough to take the Canaries through. Cheltenham: Book, Howarth, Freeman, Banks, Victory, Griffin, Yates (Jackson), Howells, Devaney (Bloomer), Grayson, McAuley (Watkins). Subs not used: Brough, Higgs.

25 August 1986

Kettering Town were defeated 3–1 at Whaddon Road in the Conference with goals from Chris Townsend, John Powell and a last-minute effort from substitute Nick Jordan. The result continued Cheltenham's encouraging start to their second season at national level.

25 August 1990

Cheltenham made the long journey to Barrow's Holker Street ground and returned with a point from a 0–0 draw against the FA Trophy holders. Cheltenham: Bartram, Crouch, Brown, Brogan, Burns, Williams, Willetts, Casey, Brain, Buckland, Tuohy. Subs: Sissons, Jordan.

25 August 1992

Mark Boyland scored his 100th goal for Cheltenham Town in a 2–2 draw with Weymouth at home. Jimmy Smith was the other scorer.

25 August 1997

Cheltenham went down 3–2 to Hereford United in the Conference, with Neil Grayson scoring twice for the Bulls at Edgar Street. Dale Watkins and Jason Eaton scored for the Robins in front of 3,704 supporters.

26 August 1989

Andy Gray made his Cheltenham Town debut in a 0–0 draw with Fisher Athletic in front of 2,200 fans.

26 August 1998

Cheltenham picked up their first win over Forest Green for eight years, winning 2–1 at the Lawn: the first three-point haul of their Conference-winning campaign. The goals came in the second half from Jason Eaton and David Norton, who netted his first for the club.

26 August 2000

Cheltenham beat Torquay United 2–0 at home, with Julian Alsop and Bob Bloomer (from the bench) both shown red cards. Jamie Victory ruptured his anterior cruciate ligament, keeping him out of action until the following season.

26 August 2006

Cheltenham beat 2004 FA Cup finalists Millwall 3–2 at Whaddon Road.

27 August 1977

Cheltenham made their return to the Premier Division of the Southern League with a 0–0 draw at home to Gravesend before 903 fans. The Robins remained unbeaten until 24 September, when they lost to Bedford Town. Cheltenham: Berry, Murphy, Foster, Dean, Dangerfield, Paterson, Hall, Paine, Thomas, Lewis, Davies. Sub: Hehir.

27 August 1988

Peter Shearer scored twice in a 3–2 win over Enfield, Steve Jenkins netting the other goal. The wonderfully talented Shearer made 26 full appearances for the Robins, scoring 7 goals.

27 August 1994

Cheltenham thrashed Corby Town 8–0 at Whaddon Road, with Jimmy Smith and Martin Boyle both scoring hat-tricks; Lee Howell and Jason Eaton being the other goalscorers. Howells opened the scoring with a thumping shot from the edge of the box in the 12th minute. Boyle made it 2–0 after a neat one-two with Smith. Jimmy Smith then scored two identical goals in the 23rd and 40th minutes, rounding the goalkeeper after through balls caught the non-existent Corby defence out. Boyle completed his hat-trick with 2 quick goals after more good work from Smith. Jason Eaton joined the action and was set up by Boyle for a goal in the 72nd minute. All that remained was for Smith to complete his treble, which he did in the 78th minute after a fine run from Howells. Corby won four games all season, ending up bottom of the table with 113 goals conceded. They did, however, hold Cheltenham to a 2–2 draw later in the season.

27 August 2001

Steve Cotterill took charge of his 200th league match as Cheltenham drew 2–2 at Swansea City's Vetch Field. It was his 275th match overall. Of a total of 200 games, the Robins won 91, losing 52 and drew the other 57. At that point the league record stood at 280 goals for, with 201 against.

28 August 1976

Cheltenham visited Barry Fry's Dunstable Town for the opening game of the season in Southern League Division One (North). The game was a thrilling 3–3 draw, with the 2 Robins goals coming from Dave Lewis, as well as one from John Reid. Cheltenham: Miles, Murphy, Scarrott, Davies, Dean, Foster, Hall, Paterson, Lewis, Hehir, Reid. Sub: McDonnell.

28 August 1982

Jimmy Gough and Steve Abbley found the target as the Robins won 2–0 at Buckingham Road, the former ground of Aylesbury United, in the Southern League Midland Division. It was Cheltenham's second win from two games at the start of their championship season.

28 August 2000

Jamie Victory's run of 158 consecutive league appearances ended against Hartlepool, due to a serious knee ligament injury picked up against Torquay United at home.

28 August 2004

Jamie Victory scored the winning goal against Boston United, for whom Paul Gascoigne came on as a second-half substitute.

29 August 1979

Cheltenham lost 2–0 at home to Alvechurch, their fourth straight defeat by the same scoreline at the start of that season. They went on to finish 19th in the Southern League Midland Division table, one place below Gloucester City.

30 August 1978

Cheltenham Town beat Telford United 2–1 with goals from John Davies and Dave Lewis. Sir Geoff Hurst was in the Telford side.

31 August 1935

Cheltenham Town played their first match in the Southern League, ending in a 5–3 win over Barry Town.

31 August 1987

Brett Angell scored his first goal for Cheltenham Town in a 1–0 win over Altrincham. He went on to score 6 goals in 5 matches.

31 August 1998

Clive Walker scored his 100th non-league goal against Barrow in a 4–1 home win, becoming the first player to score a century both inside and outside the Football League.

SEPTEMBER

1 September 1979

A Dave Lewis penalty after forty minutes earned Cheltenham Town a first qualifying round win away at Western League club Devizes Town in the FA Cup. The Robins went on to reach the third qualifier that season, where they were beaten by Merthyr Tydfil.

1 September 1984

Mark Boyland claimed a superb hat-trick as Cheltenham Town beat Folkestone Town 4–1 in the Southern League Premier Division. Ray Baverstock scored the other goal at the start of the championship-winning campaign.

1 September 2012

Cheltenham Town suffered a 3–0 home defeat by Accrington Stanley.

2 September 1989

Cheltenham Town made the trip to Runcorn's Canal Street ground and returned with an impressive 4–2 victory in the Conference. Nick Jordan, Phil Williams, Micky Nuttell and Mark Boyland were all on target for the Robins.

2 September 1995

Two late goals from Leckhampton man Guiseppe
Licata earned Cheltenham a dramatic 2–1 win at
Worcester City.

2 September 2000

Strikes from Julian Alsop and Martin Devaney earned
Cheltenham a 2–0 win at Hull City's Boothferry Park,
taking them top of League Two for the first time. It was
Alsop's first goal since arriving from Swansea City.

3 September 1975

Cheltenham were beaten 3–2 at home by Barry Town in
the Southern League Cup first-round second leg. John
Davies and Joe McDonnell scored the Cheltenham
goals, which proved crucial as the Robins progressed
courtesy of a 2–0 first leg win. Cheltenham: Berry,
Murphy, Lailey, Jones, Carroll, Gough, Skeen, Davies,
Lewis, Casey, Hall. Sub: McDonnell.

3 September 1986

Chris Townsend scored for the sixth consecutive
match from the start of the season in a 2–0 win
over Weymouth.

3 September 1996

Chris Banks, operating in midfield, scored both goals as Cheltenham beat Atherstone United 2–0 in the Dr Marten's League Premier Division. Cheltenham: Maloy, Clarke, Wring, Wotton, Freeman, Victory, Wright, Banks, Hughes, Bellingham, Howells. Subs: Bloomer, Boyle, Chenoweth.

4 September 1993

Paul Mortimore struck after an hour to earn Cheltenham a point from their away trip to Cambridge City. The home side had taken the lead at Milton Road. Cheltenham: Thomas, Bloomer, Willetts, Lovell, Clark, Iddles, Howells, Cooper, J. Smith, Hirons, Wring. Subs: Jones, Mortimore.

4 September 2011

Robins boss Mark Yates and his assistant Neil Howarth both ran the Cheltenham half marathon.

5 September 1995

Chris Robinson took charge of Cheltenham Town for the first time, overseeing a 4–0 win over Ilkeston Town.

5 September 2003

Substitute Richard Forsyth kept his head to convert two late penalties, one of which was a retake. Martin Devaney also snatched a 92nd minute winner to sink Northampton Town in a thrilling Friday night goal feast. Manager Bobby Gould had labelled his side 'The Entertainers' and on this evidence it was easy to see why. Bob Taylor was the scorer of the Robins' other goal. Cheltenham: Higgs, Griffin (Howells), Jones, M. Duff, Victory, Devaney, Cozic (Forsyth), Yates, Fyfe, Taylor, Odejayi (Brayson). Subs not used: Cleverley, Book.

6 September 1947

Cheltenham drew 2–2 with Barry Town at Whaddon Road, with Vernon Crowe and Peter Goring the goalscorers.

7 September 1985

Brian Hughes was forced to act as an emergency goalkeeper in an FA Cup first qualifying round match against Minehead. It finished 1–1. Neil Hards' car broke down en route to the match.

7 September 1997

Cheltenham played Rushden & Diamonds on a Sunday due to Princess Diana's funeral the previous day. Goals from Jason Eaton and Dale Watkins earned Cheltenham a 2–0 win in front of 1,614 fans. It was the club's 300th Conference fixture.

8 September 2001

Cheltenham lost 2–1 at Shrewsbury Town, falling 2 goals down for the fifth match in succession. Fortunately, they recovered from a slow start to win promotion that season.

9 September 1988

Shurdington-based winger Keith Knight joined Reading for £7,000, while Cheltenham signed David Craig from Bath City for £1,000.

9 September 1995

Cheltenham thrashed Yate Town 5–0 in an FA Cup first-round qualifying match, making it four big wins and 16 unanswered goals at home from the start of the season (3–0, 4–0, 4–0, 5–0).

9 September 2000

Mark Freeman made his 200th start for Cheltenham in a 1–0 defeat against Chesterfield.

10 September 1932

Cheltenham were beaten 9–3 by Redditch, with two of their goals coming from Arthur Gough and another from Jesse Goodger.

10 September 2002

Cheltenham shocked Norwich City with an amazing 3–0 win at Carrow Road in the first round of the League Cup, the undoubted highlight of Graham Allner's 32-match reign as Robins boss. Tony Naylor scored in the 30th and 45th minute, with Hugh McAuley adding the third seven minutes before full-time. Norwich included England goalkeeper Robert Green and defender Darren Kenton, who joined Cheltenham and made 15 appearances during the 2008/09 campaign. Cheltenham: Book, Howarth, Walker, Duff, Victory, McAuley, Finnigan, Yates, Milton, Alsop, Naylor. Subs not used: Higgs, Brough, Brayson, Devaney, Williams.

10 September 2011

Birmingham City and England Under-21 international loan goalkeeper Jack Butland made his Cheltenham Town debut in a 2–0 home win over Macclesfield Town.

11 September 1990

Cheltenham drew 0–0 at home with Kidderminster Harriers in front of their highest crowd of the season (1,492). Robins record signing Kim Casey appeared against his former club.

11 September 1993

Cheltenham went down 3–1 at home to Crawley Town in the Southern League. To make matters worse, there were no refreshments on offer for supporters due to a dispute with the caterers, leading Crawley fans to sing: 'Where's your tea bar gone?'

12 September 1999

Cheltenham Town's home match against Shrewsbury Town was switched to a Sunday and screened live by Sky television. The Shrews won 1–0, with Lee Steele netting the decisive goal in the 4th minute.

13 September 1967

Two goals from Joe Gadston earned Cheltenham Town a 2–0 home win over Wimbledon. They would have to wait forty-five years for another victory over the Dons at Whaddon Road.

13 September 2008

Keith Downing was sacked as Cheltenham Town manager just twenty-four hours after a 4–1 defeat at Hartlepool United.

14 September 1981

Cheltenham travelled to Penydarren Park in Merthyr Tydfil for a Southern League Midland Division clash. The Robins returned with a hard-earned 2–2 draw with first-half goals from striker Norman Pemberton and defender Tim Bayliffe. Cheltenham: Latchford, D. Berry, Bayliffe, Boxall, Dyer, Woodall, MacKenzie, Tester, Green, Pemberton, Reed. Sub: Shatford.

14 September 1985

Cheltenham suffered their first home defeat in the Conference, going down 2–1 to reigning champions Wealdstone. Mark Boyland scored the Cheltenham goal twenty minutes from time before a crowd of 982. Cheltenham: Hards, Boxall, Blackler, Collicutt, Cornes, Brooks, Hughes, Baverstock, Boyland, Abbley, Jordan. Subs: Gazzard, Brown.

14 September 2003

Cheltenham lost 3–2 at home to Bristol City despite Julian Alsop's brace, leaving them bottom of the League One table.

15 September 1976

Cheltenham thrashed Kidderminster Harriers 7–3 in Southern League Division One with Dave Lewis scoring 4 goals, the first of them a penalty. John Davies, Keiron Hehir and Steve Scarrott were also on the scoresheet in a comprehensive win at Whaddon Road. Cheltenham: N. Berry, Murphy, Scarrott, Davies, Dean, Foster, Hall, Dangerfield, Lewis, Hehir, Reid. Sub: Paterson.

15 September 1990

Cheltenham drew 2–2 with Exmouth Town in the FA Cup first qualifying round. Kevin Willetts and Chris Burns were the scorers in front of a crowd of 736. The tie went to a second replay, which Cheltenham won 3–0.

15 September 1992

Cheltenham took on Beazer Homes League Premier Division rivals Waterlooville in an FA Cup first qualifying round replay at Whaddon Road. After a 0–0 draw in the first match, the deadlock was broken by an own goal from Waterlooville's Simon Elley after fifteen minutes. Kevin Willetts hit the second goal from the penalty spot eight minutes from time.

15 September 1997

A goal from Jason Eaton two minutes from full-time earned Cheltenham a point from their first-ever visit to Hayes. The match was early in the club's first season back in the Conference, and featured a debut for on-loan Bristol Rovers defender Billy Clark.

15 September 2001

Cheltenham picked up their first win of the 2001/02 promotion season with goals from Jamie Victory and Neil Grayson, earning them a 2–0 success against Carlisle United.

15 September 2008

Martin Allen was unveiled as the new manager of Cheltenham Town.

16 September 1995

Cheltenham claimed their sixth win in a row, 2–1 at Atherstone United, to move top of the Dr Marten's League Premier Division Table.

17 September 1988

Western League Radstock Town was the venue for an FA Cup first-round qualifying-round tie. Richard Crowley and Steve Jenkins scored either side of half-time to give the Robins a 2–0 win.

17 September 2002

Cheltenham picked up their first win as a tier three club, beating Swindon Town 2–0 at Whaddon Road.

18 September 2001

Martin Devaney's goal earned Cheltenham a 1–0 win over Hartlepool United.

19 September 1936

Cheltenham beat Weston-super-Mare 13–3 in an FA Cup preliminary round tie at Whaddon Road. The goals were scored by Green (3), Collett (6), Ray (3) and Brae.

19 September 1990

Cheltenham drew their replay 3–3 at Exmouth, with the Robins fans at the game becoming known as the 'Exmouth 18'. The crowd was 288.

19 September 1998

Cheltenham registered their seventh straight victory, 3–0 over Southport at home with Clive Walker scoring the pick of the goals.

19 September 2006

Cheltenham took the lead at West Bromwich Albion in the second round of the League Cup through Kayode Odejayi, but the Baggies hit back to progress with a 3–1 win.

20 September 2005

John Ward's Cheltenham took Premier League Sunderland to extra time at the Stadium of Light in the second round of the League Cup, but the Black Cats eventually won 1–0 thanks to Anthony Le Tallac's goal.

21 September 1935

Cheltenham beat Paulton Rovers 4–0, with Ernest Coombs helping himself to a hat-trick and Frederick Jones netting the other goal in an FA Cup preliminary round tie.

22 September 1962

Danny Mitchinson scored a hat-trick in a 5–1 win over Lovells Athletic; Calland and Shepperley also scored. It was the fourth game in a row that Mitchinson had scored after coming back from a long absence due to injury.

22 September 1998

Cheltenham moved top of the Conference table for the first time after a 1–1 home draw with Woking. Rushden's match at Leek Town was abandoned due to a fire at a nearby chemical factory.

22 September 2008

Martin Allen transfer listed six players: Jerry Gill, Craig Armstrong, Andy Lindegaard, Lee Ridley, Josh Low and Aaron Ledgister.

23 September 1933

Cheltenham beat Birmingham Trams 5–1 with 2 goals each from Horace Payne and George Knight, as well as one from George Blackburn.

23 September 1988

Cheltenham signed Micky Tanner from Bath City.

23 September 2000

Martin Devaney scored Cheltenham's first Football League hat-trick in a 5–2 home win over Plymouth Argyle. Antony Griffin and Lee Howells were the other scorers. It was Griffin's first Cheltenham goal, and the first time Cheltenham had scored four or more in the Football League.

24 September 1990

Cheltenham finally ousted Exmouth 3–0 in a second replay, with goals from Kim Casey, Mickey Nuttell and Phil Williams. Robins boss Jim Barron signed four Exmouth players (Tony Stuart, Mike Barrett, Frank Howarth and Mark Gennard) on the back of their performances in the three matches against Cheltenham.

24 September 1996

Michael Duff made his Cheltenham Town debut in a 1–1 home draw with Dorchester Town in front of 536 fans, Jamie Victory scored the Robins' goal.

24 September 2008

Cheltenham signed young duo Josh Payne and Lewis Montrose on loan from West Ham United and Wigan Athletic respectively.

25 September 1993

Ian Weston scored on his Cheltenham Town debut in a 1–1 draw against Farnborough Town. Weston went on to become the club's sports therapist in 2002.

26 September 2008

Cheltenham Town signed Stuart Fleetwood on loan from Charlton Athletic.

27 September 2008

Stuart Fleetwood scored on his debut in a 2–2 home draw with Stockport County, which was Jerry Gill's last appearance for the club. Josh Payne also scored on his debut.

28 September 1991

Cheltenham thrashed Taunton Town 8–0 in the FA Cup second qualifying round, with goals from Kevin Willetts, Loy Stobart, Mark Buckland, Kim Casey (3) and Nick Jordan (2). Cheltenham were dumped out 4–0 by Weymouth in the next round.

28 September 1996

Jason Eaton scored a hat-trick in Cheltenham Town's 4–3 FA Cup second-round qualifying match against Salisbury City.

29 September 1979

Former Southampton player Bobby Stokes made his Cheltenham Town debut against Cambridge City. He went on to make 18 starts, scoring twice.

29 September 1997

Dale Watkins scored twice at Aggborough as Cheltenham beat Kidderminster Harriers 2–1 in front of 2,320 fans.

30 September 1989

Cheltenham hit Weston-super-Mare for seven in the FA Cup second qualifying round. The goals came from Nick Jordan, Steve Brooks, Mark Buckland (3), Kevin Willetts and Mark Boyland.

OCTOBER

1 October 1977

Duncan Edwards made his Cheltenham Town debut as a substitute in a 2–1 win over Nuneaton. He went on to make nearly 100 first team starts, scoring once.

1 October 1978

Cheltenham signed Graham McKenzie from Wycombe, John Dyer from Redditch and Keith Hardcastle from Bristol City.

1 October 1988

John Murphy resigned after a 3–0 FA Cup defeat at Gloucester City, their first there since 1928/29.

1 October 1991

Cheltenham lost 5–1 at Bath City, with Mark Buckland scoring their consolation goal.

1 October 1994

Cheltenham moved top of the Beazer Homes League Premier Division with an emphatic 5–1 win at Sudbury Town's Priory ground. The goals came from Lee Howells, Martin Boyle (2), Andy Tucker and Chris Banks.

2 October 1965

Cheltenham beat Devizes Town 8–2 in the FA Cup third qualifying round, with Gerald Horlick claiming a hat-trick. He finished the season with 24 goals.

2 October 1982

Cheltenham found themselves in the unusual position of being a division below county rivals Gloucester City during the 1982/83 season, but Alan Wood's side had a chance to upset the Tigers in an FA Cup second qualifying round tie at Whaddon Road. They did so emphatically, winning 5–1 with goals from Steve Abbley, John Dyer, Dave Lewis (2) and Jimmy Gough. Cheltenham: Ogden, Dyer, Murphy, Cornes, Ryan, Paterson, Scarrott, Pemberton (Tester), Lewis, Gough, Abbley.

2 October 2002

Cheltenham lost 7–0 at Crystal Palace in the second round of the League Cup at Selhurst Park.

2 October 2007

John Ward resigned as Cheltenham Town manager to take the top job at Carlisle United. He had taken charge of 205 matches, winning 75, drawing 53 and losing 77. He made the announcement immediately after a 3–0 defeat at Port Vale. He had guided Cheltenham to their highest-ever finish of 17th in League One the previous season.

3 October 1987

Chris Townsend was on target for the Robins as they drew 1–1 with Enfield in the Conference before a crowd of 1,409. Paul Furlong, who went on to play for Chelsea and Birmingham City, scored his first-ever senior goal for Enfield in the match at Whaddon Road.

3 October 1998

Cheltenham Town drew 1–1 at home to Dover Athletic in their Conference title-winning season. A crowd of 2,575 saw Neil Grayson secure a point with a 66th minute equaliser after the visitors had taken the lead though Ricky Reina two minutes earlier.

3 October 2009

Cheltenham Town drew 1–1 at home to Notts County, with former England boss Sven Goran Eriksson in the Whaddon Road stand in his director of football capacity for the League Two club.

4 October 1919

Cheltenham played their first ever FA Cup match, away to Chippenham Town. It ended in a 4–0 defeat.

4 October 2008

Cheltenham drew 3–3 with Brighton in a thrilling match at the Withdean Stadium. Scott Murray scored twice, with Andy Gallinagh's late effort rescuing a point for Martin Allen's team.

5 October 1935

Cheltenham enjoyed an 8–1 win over Purton Athletic in the FA Cup, with Ernest Coombs scoring 6 of the goals.

5 October 1974

Dave Lewis scored his 100th Cheltenham goal in a 4–1 win over Gloucester City in the FA Cup second qualifying round at Whaddon Road.

5 October 1977

Cheltenham lost 2–0 at home to Hillingdon Borough in the Southern League Premier Division in front of a crowd of 1,042.

5 October 1982

Norman Pemberton and Steve Scarrott found the net as the Robins achieved a 2–1 victory at Witney Town's old Marriott's Close ground in the Southern League Cup second round. They went on to reach the semi-finals before losing to eventual winners Alvechurch. Cheltenham: Ogden, Ryan, Dyer, Murphy, Cornes, Paterson, Scarrott, Pemberton, Gough, Lewis, Abbley. Sub: Tester.

5 October 1991

Cheltenham hit back from a goal down to beat Redbridge Forest 2–1 thanks to a late double from Mark Buckland in the 87th and 90th minutes. It earned the Robins their first away win of the season.

5 October 1994

Jason Eaton struck from the penalty spot ten minutes before half-time, resulting in Cheltenham winning 1–0 at Yate Town in the Southern League Cup first round. The Robins finished runners-up in the Premier Division that year and reached the quarter-finals of the League Cup.

5 October 1999

Cheltenham were beaten 1–0 by Kingstonian in the Conference Championship Shield at Whaddon Road.

5 October 2001

Tony Naylor opened his scoring account for Cheltenham in a 2–1 home win over Lincoln City.

6 October 1998

Cheltenham lost 1–0 to Halifax Town in the Conference Championship Shield at Whaddon Road.

6 October 2006

Cheltenham ended a run of six straight defeats with a 1–0 win at Yeovil Town. J.J. Melligan scored the all-important goal.

6 October 2007

Keith Downing took charge of his first game as caretaker manager, which ended in a 1–1 home draw with Oldham Athletic. Michael Townsend scored Cheltenham's goal, while teammate Jerry Gill was sent off.

7 October 1995

Darren Wright made his Cheltenham debut in a 2–0 home win over Gresley Rovers, with Jimmy Smith scoring both goals.

8 October 1932

Cheltenham beat Cannock Town 7–1 with 2 goals each from Billy Vaughan and Arthur Gough, one apiece from Eric Mason and Pat Collins and an own goal. They lost the return match 2–1, with Gough on target again.

8 October 1994

Cheltenham beat VS Rugby 1–0 at home in controversial circumstances, with the visitors seeing a shot which clearly hit the stanchion inside the goal and bounced out not given.

8 October 2004

Liverpool and Wales legend Ian Rush brought his Chester City side to Whaddon Road, with the match finishing goalless.

8 October 2007

Ex-Aston Villa and Blackburn Rovers left-back Alan Wright signed non-contract terms with Cheltenham Town.

9 October 1996

Bob Bloomer donned the goalkeeping gloves for Cheltenham Town in a Dr Marten's Cup first-round first-leg match at Newport AFC, after Ryan Gannaway was sent off thirty-five minutes into his debut.

9 October 2001

Defender Keith Hill joined Wrexham on loan, having failed to break into Cheltenham's first-team picture.

10 October 2009

Cheltenham were humiliated 4–0 at Accrington Stanley, with 5ft 5in midfielder Sam Cox asked to fill in at centre-half on his nineteenth birthday.

11 October 1997

Cheltenham beat Paulton Rovers 5–0 at home in the FA Cup third qualifying round. Jimmy Smith made his 250th appearance and scored his 121st goal for the club. Dale Watkins, Bob Bloomer and Mark Crisp were also on the scoresheet, along with an own goal.

11 October 2003

Cheltenham unveiled a new blue and black kit, but went down 3–1 at Boston United, with striker Damian Spencer forced to take over in goal after Steve Book was sent off.

12 October 1957

Cheltenham Town lost 6–2 at Worcester City. Their scorers were Clive Burder and Sid Dunn.

13 October 2007

Kris Commons helped himself to a hat-trick as Cheltenham were beaten 3–0 at home by Nottingham Forest.

14 October 1995

Jimmy Smith's brace earned Cheltenham Town a 2–1 win at Cambridge City's Milton Road in the Premier Division of the Dr Marten's League.

15 October 1985

Kevin Willetts made his debut at Wycombe Wanderers, scoring at both ends in a 3–3 draw. Steve Brooks and Steve Abbey were the other scorers at Loakes Park.

15 October 1988

Cheltenham beat Kidderminster Harriers 4–1 at home with goals from Steve Brooks, Nick Jordan, Kevin Willetts and Micky Tanner in front of 1,308 fans.

15 October 1994

Cheltenham drew a friendly match 1–1 at home to Wokingham, with Christer Warren netting their goal. Tragically, Wokingham's Elliot Pearce was killed in a car crash on his way home from the game.

16 October 1990

Robins manager Jim Barron was not offered a new contract, and was dismissed the next day.

16 October 2009

Martin Allen took charge of Cheltenham for the final time for a 2–1 home defeat by Macclesfield Town. He was placed on gardening leave for an alleged nightclub incident four days later.

17 October 1995

Jimmy Smith scored two first-half goals as Cheltenham defeated Weston-super-Mare 4–2 in the Dr Marten's Cup first-round second leg. Leading 2–1 from the first leg, the Robins cruised through with Steve Jones and Giuseppe Licata also on target.

17 October 1998

A scrambled goal from Jason Eaton was enough to earn Cheltenham a 1–0 win at Barnstaple Town in the FA Cup third qualifying round. Cheltenham: Book, Duff, Victory, Banks, Knight, Brough, Howells, C. Walker, Eaton, Grayson, Norton.

17 October 2000

Grant McCann joined Cheltenham on loan from West Ham and sat on the bench as an unused substitute in a 2–1 win at Halifax Town.

18 October 1986

Cheltenham were beaten 2–0 at Altrincham, who were one of the strongest teams in non-league football at the time.

18 October 2003

Bobby Gould resigned immediately after a 2–0 home defeat by Rochdale, with the fans calling for him to quit. Cheltenham were 19th in the table after their relegation the previous season. His overall record as boss stood at just 9 wins from 36 games; the Robins had lost 14 and drawn the remaining 13.

19 October 1985

Cheltenham enjoyed a 5–1 win over Kettering Town, with Brian Hughes netting twice from the spot, Mark Boyland bagging a brace and Neil Smith getting the other in front of 1,221 fans.

20 October 1990

Cheltenham bounced back from Conference defeats by Colchester United and Barnet with a 2–2 home draw against Macclesfield Town. Goals in each half from Mark Buckland and Chris Burns were enough to earn a point.

20 October 1999

Martin Devaney broke a bone in his foot in a reserve match against Hereford United, keeping him out of action until January 2000.

20 October 2009

Martin Allen was placed on gardening leave by Cheltenham Town following an alleged nightclub incident.

21 October 1978

Dave Lewis scored twice as Cheltenham defeated Trowbridge Town 4–0 in the FA Cup third qualifying round. John Dyer and Keith Hardcastle scored the other goals to send the Robins into a home fourth qualifier against Yeovil Town. Cheltenham: Miles, Murphy, Edwards, Foster, Dean, Brown, MacKenzie, Dyer, Lewis, Davies, Hardcastle.

21 October 1989

Nick Jordan and Andy Gray scored the goals as Cheltenham defeated Chorley 2–0 at Whaddon Road in front of 1,308 fans. It was Gray's first goal for the club. Cheltenham: Mogg, Baverstock, Willetts, Crowley, Vircavs, Williams, Brooks, Sanderson, Jordan, Buckland, Gray.

21 October 2008

Australian midfielder James Wesolowski suffered a broken leg in a defeat at Tranmere Rovers, cutting short his loan spell from Leicester City.

22 October 1983

Cheltenham scored 3 goals for the second successive league game as Dartford were beaten 3–0 at Whaddon Road in the Premier Division of the Southern League. Stuart Cornes opened the scoring after sixteen minutes and there were 2 goals in as many minutes for Norman Pemberton and Terry Paterson midway through the second half.

22 October 1998

Cheltenham Town signed left-sided defender Richard Walker from Hereford United for a five-figure sum. His time at Whaddon Road was blighted by injuries, but he did shine in the 2002 play-off final victory over Rushden & Diamonds.

23 October 2001

Jamie Victory scored both goals as Cheltenham drew 2–2 at Rochdale, with goalkeeper Steve Book dropping a clanger, to allow Dale back into the match. Boss Steve Cotterill threw Book's tracksuit across the changing room after the game, smashing his watch – he later paid to have it repaired.

24 October 1992

Cheltenham Town signed Jason Eaton from Gloucester City for a fee of £15,000 and he went on to become the third-highest scorer in the club's history.

24 October 1998

Cheltenham beat Doncaster Rovers 2–1 in Steve Cotterill's 100th match in charge. Michael Duff scored his first goal for the club. Under Cotterill, the Robins had won 55 games, drawn 27 and lost just 18. Their goal record stood at 169 for, with 96 against.

25 October 1994

Cheltenham were knocked out of the FA Cup 2–1 by Bashley in a fourth qualifying round replay. Neil Smith's goal was not enough to avoid a Cup disappointment.

25 October 1997

Keith Knight's goal was enough to knock Sutton United out of the FA Cup in the fourth qualifying round at Whaddon Road. Cheltenham: Book, Duff, Victory, Banks, Freeman, Smith, Howells, Knight, Eaton, Watkins, Bloomer.

26 October 1935

Cheltenham beat Evesham United 7–1 in the Worcestershire Senior Cup first round.

26 October 1996

Cheltenham drew 0–0 at Bath City's Twerton Park in the FA Cup fourth qualifying round.

27 October 1984

Cheltenham suffered a rare defeat in their Southern League title-winning season, going down 3–1 to Shepshed Charterhouse. Clive Boxall scored the Robins' only goal. Cheltenham: Martyn, Murphy, Paterson, Collicutt, Boxall, Jordan, Hughes, Baverstock, Boyland, Wright, Burford.

27 October 2011

Whaddon Road hosted an Under-16 Victory Shield match between England and Wales, which the young Three Lions won 4–0.

28 October 1980

Chris Gardner scored four minutes from time to earn Cheltenham a point at Wellingborough Town. Only 120 gathered at the Dog & Duck to see the Southern League Midland Division fixture. Cheltenham: Harris, Pemberton, Dyer, Hardcastle, Hams, Kavanagh, McKenzie, Gardner, Buckland, Boxall, Shatford.

28 October 1992

Jason Eaton made his Cheltenham Town debut in a 1–0 win at Weymouth, with Steve Brown scoring the winner. Eaton went on to net 115 goals for Cheltenham.

28 October 1995

Jimmy Smith scored after sixteen seconds against former club Salisbury City in a 3–3 draw. Jason Eaton and Darren Wright were the other scorers.

28 October 2006

Cheltenham lost 2–0 at home to Nottingham Forest, Nicky Southall scoring both of the former European Champions' goals.

29 October 1977

Cheltenham drew 3–3 with Kettering Town in a thrilling game at Whaddon Road in the Southern League Premier Division. Dave Lewis scored twice, with one from Ray Dean. Cheltenham: N. Berry, Murphy, Dangerfield, Foster, Dean, Paterson, Rice, D. Berry, Davies, Lewis, Gardner.

29 October 1994

Cheltenham thrashed Hastings Town 6–0 with Jason Eaton scoring a hat-trick. They were averaging 3 goals per game at that point in the season. Jimmy Smith, Simon Cooper and Martin Boyle were the other scorers. The result took Cheltenham top of the league on goal difference ahead of eventual champions Hednesford Town. Cheltenham: Thomas, Tucker, Bloomer, Banks, Jones, N. Smith, Howells (Warren), Cooper, J. Smith, Boyle, Eaton. Subs not used: Lovell, Cook.

29 October 1996

Cheltenham hit back from a goal down to beat Bath City 4–1 during extra time in their fourth qualifying round replay, earning a trip to Peterborough United in the first round proper. Lee Howells scored his 50th Cheltenham goal, with Martin Boyle, Jimmy Smith and Jason Eaton the other scorers. Cheltenham had numerous early chances, but Mike Davis put Bath ahead in the 35th minute. The Romans then defended stoutly, with their back four including former Robin Richard Crowley. The breakthrough finally came in the 90th minute, when substitute Boyle stooped to head home against his former club. Bath were visibly deflated and Cheltenham ran riot in extra time. Cheltenham: Maloy, Wotton, Wring, Banks, Freeman (Boyle), Victory, Howells, Wright, Eaton, Smith, Clarke (Bloomer). Sub not used: Gannaway.

30 October 1993

First-half goals from Neil Smith and Jason Eaton earned the Robins their first away win of the season – a 2–1 success against Solihull Borough. Goalkeeper Martin Thomas played a big part in the Southern League Premier Division win with a series of second-half saves.

30 October 1998

Steve Cotterill had a bid for Morecambe striker John Norman turned down, with the Merseyside-based player not keen on the travelling the move would have involved.

30 October 2001

Cheltenham were knocked out of the LDV Vans Trophy 5–4 on penalties at Cambridge United after a 1–1 draw at the Abbey Stadium.

31 October 1988

Jim Barron was appointed player/manager of Cheltenham Town.

31 October 2009

Cheltenham lost 4–0 at home to Crewe Alexandra.

NOVEMBER

1 November 1933

Cheltenham lost 2–1 to Llanelli after a replay in the third qualifying round of the FA Cup, only to be given a reprieve as the Welsh club were thrown out of the competition for fielding an ineligible player. Cheltenham went on to reach the third round proper for the first time.

1 November 1997

Jason Eaton scored an eleven-minute hat-trick in a 4–0 win over previously undefeated Conference leaders Halifax Town at Whaddon Road, ending their 12-match unbeaten run. The match pitted the oldest manager in the Conference, George Mulhall, against the youngest, Steve Cotterill. Bob Bloomer scored Cheltenham's other goal with a cracking left-footed finish. Cheltenham: Book, Duff, Victory, Banks, Freeman, Smith (Benton), Howells, Knight, Eaton (Wright), Watkins (Crisp), Bloomer.

1 November 1999

Former Blackburn Rovers player Nicky Marker joined Cheltenham Town, but he left without making a first team appearance.

2 November 1935

Cheltenham registered their record cup victory, thrashing Chippenham Rovers 12–0 in the FA Cup third qualifying round. Cheltenham: Bowles, Whitehouse, Williams, Lang, Devonport, Partridge, Perkins, Hackett, Jones, Black, Griffiths. James Black and Frederick Jones each scored four times in the rout.

2 November 1996

Cheltenham enjoyed a 6–0 home win over Ashford Town in the Dr Marten's League Premier Division. Jamie Victory and Lee Howells both scored twice, with Jimmy Smith and Martin Boyle also contributing to the final score.

2 November 2004

Cheltenham lost 4–3 on penalties to Paul Merson's Walsall in the LDV Vans Trophy after a 2–2 draw at Whaddon Road. Steve Guinan and John Brough scored the goals for Cheltenham.

2 November 2010

Cheltenham were leading 1–0 at home to Southend United thanks to J.J. Melligan's goal, but floodlight failure due an electrical fire saw the game abandoned. Southend won the rearranged match 2–0.

3 November 1962

Cheltenham were beaten 6–3 by Enfield in an FA Cup first qualifying round match, their goals coming from Allan Palmer, Danny Mitchinson and Bobby McCool.

3 November 2001

Cheltenham suffered their heaviest defeat since 1992, going down 5–1 at Hull City, but boss Steve Cotterill remained adamant he would not swap any of his players for Hull's. He was proved correct as Cheltenham went on to win promotion that season. Julian Alsop scored Cheltenham's only goal at Boothferry Park.

3 November 2007

Keith Downing's first match as full-time boss ended in a disappointing 2–0 defeat at Walsall in League One.

4 November 2000

Chris Banks scored his one and only Football League goal for Cheltenham Town in a 1–1 draw at Kidderminster Harriers. It was his first since April 1989, when he struck for Exeter City, a match which he finished as the emergency goalkeeper. Michael Jackson made his first Football League start for Cheltenham at Aggborough.

5 November 1977

Goals at each end of the game – from Ray Dean after five minutes and Dave Lewis six minutes from time – earned Cheltenham a 2–1 victory over Dover.

5 November 1988

A strong Barnet side won 2–1 at Whaddon Road, despite Steve Brooks putting Cheltenham ahead after thirty minutes. Cheltenham: Mogg, Whelan, Willetts, Crouch, Burns, Shearer, Brooks, Tanner, Jenkins, Buckland, Jordan.

5 November 2011

Cheltenham picked up their first ever win at Bradford City, with Kaid Mohamed's goal enough to earn 3 points at Valley Parade.

6 November 1985

Maidstone United visited Whaddon Road in the Bob Lord Trophy, winning 3–2. Cheltenham's goals came from Kevin Willetts and Nigel Smith and there were 874 there to see it. Cheltenham: Hards, Baverstock, Blackler, Boxall, Cornes, Brooks, Hughes, Smith, Boyland, Abbley, Willetts.

6 November 1997

Clive Walker joined Cheltenham Town from Brentford, where he was assistant manager.

6 November 2001

The new Wymans Road stand opened for the visit of Bristol Rovers, the Robins' first league match against the Gas since 1938, when they played against the reserve team. The game finished goalless.

6 November 2003

John Ward was named as Cheltenham Town manager, succeeding Bobby Gould. Alan McDonald and Steve Perryman were the other men interviewed for the position.

7 November 1981

A crowd of only 200 people watched Cheltenham play Barry Town at Jenner Park, where the home side triumphed 2–0.

7 November 1992

Two goals from Jimmy Smith and one from Jason Eaton earned Cheltenham a 3–1 win over Dorchester Town. Cheltenham: Nicholls, Lovell, Willetts, Brown, Vircavs, Tucker, Wring, N. Smith, J. Smith, Eaton, Hirons.

7 November 1998

Cheltenham lost 1–0 at Woking, with Clive Walker missing a penalty against his old club. They went on a run of 692 minutes without conceding a goal after that match, taking them up to 9 January 1999, when they drew 2–2 at Doncaster Rovers.

8 November 1969

Cheltenham's first ever FA Trophy tie ended in an 8–0 win over St Blazey. The goals were scored by Gerald Horlick (2), Henry Wiggin (2), Tony Cooper (2) and Ralph Norton (2). They went on to defeat Ton Pentre and Gloucester City, but lost to Romford in the first round proper. The match was watched by a crowd of 1,129.

8 November 1980

Graham MacKenzie scored the only Cheltenham goal in a 2–1 defeat at Merthyr Tydfil, the second of three consecutive away defeats in the Southern League Midland Division. Cheltenham: Harris, Buckland, Dyer, Hardcastle, Hams, Kavanagh, MacKenzie, Gardner, Pemberton, Boxall, Shatford.

8 November 1997

Clive Walker made his Cheltenham Town debut as a substitute at Slough Town in Cheltenham's 2–1 victory courtesy of goals from Lee Howells and Dale Watkins.

8 November 2003

John Ward took charge of his first match, a 3–1 FA Cup win over Hull City.

9 November 1962

Willie Ferns signed for Cheltenham Town from Hamilton Academical.

9 November 1946

Cheltenham won 5–2 against a Polish Army XI, with Vernon Crowe scoring a hat-trick.

9 November 1999

The Robins travelled to Gillingham for an FA Cup first-round replay. The home side took a 2–0 lead, but spectacular strikes from Russell Milton and Neil Howarth levelled the scores, only for Brian McGlinchey to beat Steve Book with a deflected shot to take the Gills through. Cheltenham: Book, Howarth, Freeman, Banks, Victory, Duff, Yates, Howells, Milton, Brough, McAuley.

9 November 2001

Mark Yates was sent off for two yellow cards in Cheltenham Town's 0–0 home draw with Plymouth Argyle.

10 November 1976

Ray Dean and Kieron Hehir were on target in a 2–1 win for Cheltenham at Milton Keynes City.

10 November 1979

Southampton legend Terry Paine resigned as Cheltenham Town manager. He had combined his role with running the Prince of Wales pub in the town centre.

10 November 1983

Steve Scarrott was released after 95 appearances and 12 goals for Cheltenham.

10 November 1984

Cheltenham's Southern League championship season featured an alarming dip in form during the autumn, suffering the third of four consecutive defeats against Crawley Town. The Robins' goal was an own goal from Crawley defender Andy Coghill. Cheltenham: Martyn, Boxall, Paterson, Collicutt, Cornes, Jordan, Hughes, Baverstock, Boyland, Wright, Burford.

10 November 1990

Cheltenham entered the Welsh Cup for a brief spell and visited Welsh League side Cwmbran Town in the third round. They won the game 7–1 with goals from Mark Buckland, Mick Tuohy (2), Simon Brain (2), Kim Casey and Chris Burns. Cwmbran's goal was scored by ex-Robins player Neil Goff. Cheltenham: Barrett, Stuart, Willetts, Brogan, Gennard, Bloomfield, Burns, Casey, Brain, Buckland, Tuohy.

11 November 1933

Cheltenham beat Calne and Harris United 10–1 in the FA Cup fourth qualifying round. The goals came from Yarwood (4), Blackburn, Knight (2), Hill (2) and Hazard.

11 November 1985

Cheltenham beat Gloucester City 7–1 in the Gloucestershire Senior Cup. The scorers were Steve Brooks (2), Chris Townsend, Brian Hughes, Steve Abbley, Stuart Cornes and an own goal.

11 November 1995

Second-half goals from Jimmy Wring and Jimmy Smith earned Cheltenham Town a 2–0 win over newly-promoted Newport AFC.

12 November 2011

Cheltenham gave League One Tranmere Rovers a shock in the first round of the FA Cup at Prenton Park, with Darryl Duffy scoring the winner from the penalty spot. Martin Devaney went on as a substitute for Tranmere against his hometown club, but he was unable to create an equaliser.

13 November 1976

Cheltenham enjoyed an 8–0 win over Bedworth United, with 2 goals apiece from Ray Bishop and Chris Gardner. John Davies, Kieron Hehir, a Dave Dangerfield penalty and an own goal also contributed to the final score. The attendance was 495.

13 November 2001

Michael Duff played for Northern Ireland against Macclesfield Town in a Sammy McIlroy tribute match at Moss Rose, paving the way for his international career that has spanned more than 20 caps.

14 November 1959

Cheltenham held Watford to a 0–0 draw in the FA Cup first round, going down 3–0 in the replay in front of 11,481 fans.

14 November 1987

Cheltenham took an early lead at Wolves in the first round of the FA Cup, but the Football League side ran out 5–1 winners. The only time Cheltenham had played Wolves prior to this encounter was a friendly to baptise the new Whaddon Road floodlights in October 1951. Brett Angell gave them the lead with a sweet strike after twenty minutes and an upset seemed possible, but their hopes faded quickly. Nigel Vaughan levelled for Wolves and Steve Bull showed his goalscoring power with a hat-trick. Their other scorer was Keith Downing, who went on to manage Cheltenham in 2007/08. Ally Robertson was also in the Wolves side, another future Robins boss. Cheltenham: Churchward, Buckland, Vircavs, Crowley, Willetts, Hughes, Baverstock, Brown, Brooks, Angell, Boyland. Subs not used: Jordan, Townsend.

14 November 1992

Southern League Cheltenham knocked out Isthmian League St Albans 2–1 in the FA Cup first round to set up a home tie with Bournemouth in round two. The right foot of Jon Purdie connected with a cross from Jimmy Smith on the left for the winning goal in the 72nd minute of a magical match for the Robins, played on a perfect pitch which was used by England for training. Cheltenham then defied eighteen minutes of hell from St Albans before celebrating as they reached the second round of the FA Cup for the first time since 1947/48. Martin Duffield had put St Albans ahead in the 56th minute with a penalty after a foul by seventeen-year-old Andy Tucker. Kevin Willetts calmly converted from the spot after substitute Purdie had been tripped and Purdie won it. There were 3,189 in attendance. Cheltenham: Nicholls, Howells, Willetts, Brown, Vircavs, Tucker, Lovell, N. Smith, J. Smith, Bloomer, Hirons (Purdie).

14 November 1998

A second-half goal from Lee Thorpe settled the FA Cup first-round tie between Cheltenham of the Conference and Lincoln of League One. A crowd of 3,589, plus the BBC *Match of the Day* cameras were present in the hope of seeing a shock result.

15 November 1986

Cheltenham beat Northwich Victoria 5–2 at home with goals from Mark Boyland (2), Brian Hughes (2) and Steve Brooks. Attendance: 1,017.

15 November 1997

Cheltenham knocked Tiverton Town out of the FA Cup thanks to Clive Walker's late winner, his first goal for the Robins. Jason Eaton was the other scorer in a 2–1 victory en route to a first appearance in the third round proper since 1933/34.

15 November 2008

Cheltenham suffered a humiliating 3–0 defeat at Hereford United in what was Shane Higgs' final appearance in goal; Steve Guinan scored twice against his old club. Manager Martin Allen had the team coach pulled over in a layby on the way home and told his players what he thought of their performance.

16 November 1996

Cheltenham claimed a creditable 0–0 draw at Peterborough United in the FA Cup first round. Peterborough dominated the early stages and they were awarded a penalty when Chris Banks was adjudged to have tripped Scott Houghton. Martin O'Connor, who was being watched by Birmingham City, fluffed his spot kick wide of Kevin Maloy's right-hand post. Cheltenham grew in confidence and Jamie Victory hit the post with a header from Lee Howells' corner late on. Cheltenham: Maloy, Wotton (Bloomer), Wring, Banks, Freeman, Victory, Banks, Freeman, Howells, Wright, Boyle (Eaton), Smith (Chenoweth), Clarke.

17 November 1956

The largest crowd ever assembled at Whaddon Road saw Arch Anderson's Cheltenham play Reading in the FA Cup first round. The figure of 8,326 was more than 2,000 higher than the previous record of 6,000 for Cardiff City's visit. Cheltenham went down fighting, with Jim McAllister putting them ahead in the 15th minute and Joe Hyde producing a colossal display at centre half. But 2 goals from Dixon were enough to take the Royals through. The previous season had seen Cheltenham finish second in the Southern League – the highest position they had achieved, but not since they played Blackpool twenty-two years earlier had there been such interest in a Robins game. Cheltenham: Gourlay, McDonald, Baird, Farrel, Hyde, Dunn, Cleland, Scott, McAllister, Keen, Burder.

17 November 1990

Conference club Cheltenham were knocked out of the FA Cup 1–0 at Birmingham City's St Andrews before a crowd of 7,942. They may have lost, but they earned the respect of the Blues fans and staff alike after a gallant fight against their League One-level opponents. It took the pass of the match to break Cheltenham in the 57th minute, and the man who scored was Simon Sturridge, the only player who had more speed than they could handle. He was set up by Nigel Gleghorn after Greg Downs had dispossessed Miguel de Souza near his own penalty area. Sturridge raced onto the 60-yard ball and beat guest goalkeeper Steve Weaver with a brilliant finish to spare Birmingham's blushes. Cheltenham: Weaver, de Souza (Crouch), Willetts, Brogan, Vircavs, Jordan, Burns, Brain, Casey, Buckland, Tuohy. Subs not used: Hancox.

17 November 2001

Cheltenham fell behind to non-league Kettering Town, but they stormed back to win 6–1 and book their place in the second round of the FA Cup. Their scorers were Tony Naylor and Julian Alsop (with 2 goals each), Lee Howells and Martin Devaney. Darren Collins missed a golden chance to put Kettering 2–0 up before Cheltenham began their fight back. Ex-Robins front runner Dale Watkins was in the Poppies team.

18 November 1989

Andy Gray scored both goals in a 2–0 win at Chorley in front of 587 fans. Cheltenham: Beasley, Whelan, Willetts, Crowley, Vircavs, Williams, Brooks, Mardenborough, Jordan, Buckland, Gray.

18 November 2000

Cheltenham beat Shrewsbury Town 4–1 in the FA Cup first round, their first win over League opposition since 1933 when they beat Carlisle United. The goals came from Lee Howells, Neil Grayson (2) and Julian Alsop.

19 November 1994

Cheltenham lost 3–1 at Hastings Town, whom they had thrashed 6–0 at home three weeks earlier. Their only goal was scored by a Hastings player.

19 November 1998

John Ward took a guest training session for Steve Cotterill's Robins. He went on to manage the club from 2003 to 2007.

20 November 1982

A goal from Paul Tester after eight minutes earned Cheltenham a 1–0 home win over Bromsgrove Rovers. It was the third of eight consecutive wins on the way to the league title.

20 November 1993

Cheltenham thrashed Atherstone United 5–1 at home with goals from Lee Howells, Bob Bloomer, Jason Eaton and Jimmy Smith (2). Cheltenham: Thomas, Bloomer, S. Jones, Tucker, N. Smith, V. Jones, Howells, Owen, J. Smith, Eaton, Warren.

20 November 2001

Cheltenham enjoyed a 4–1 home win over Macclesfield Town, with Lee Williams, Michael Duff and Julian Alsop on target along with an own goal.

21 November 1970

Cheltenham Town lost 4–0 to Brighton & Hove Albion in the first round of the FA Cup at the Goldstone Ground. The crowd was 8,348. They beat Burton in the fourth qualifying round 3–0 in a replay, after a 2–2 draw at Whaddon Road. Cheltenham: Heeks, Thorndale, Corboy, Amos, Jefferies, Etheridge, Cooper, Lewis, Crosbie, Fraser, Wilkes. Sub: White.

22 November 1978

Cheltenham drew 0–0 with Yeovil Town at the club's old Huish ground. The match took place in the Southern League Premier Division with Cheltenham trying (unsuccessfully) to qualify for the inaugural season of the Alliance Premier League (now Blue Square Bet Premier). Cheltenham: Miles, Murphy, Dangerfield, Foster, Dean, Brown, MacKenzie, Dyer, Lewis, Davies, Hardcastle.

22 November 1986

Despite heavy mud and driving rain, Cheltenham and Gateshead served up an entertaining match won 4–2 by the Robins. Chris Townsend's 2 goals, a fine individual effort from Steve Brooks and a Brian Hughes penalty decided the result. Cheltenham: Hards, Baverstock, Willetts, Collicutt, Vircavs, Brooks, Powell, Townsend, Boyland, Hughes, Jordan.

22 November 1997

Bob Bloomer made his 200th Cheltenham Town appearance against Gateshead.

22 November 2007

Cameroonian Guy Madjo and Canadian Michael D'Agostino joined Cheltenham on loan deadline day.

23 November 1999

Neil Grayson scored one of the most spectacular goals Whaddon Road has ever seen, volleying in from 40 yards against Plymouth Argyle. He also scored the opening goal in a 2–0 win for Steve Cotterill's side.

23 November 2006

Cheltenham Town signed experienced midfielder Kristian O'Leary on loan from Swansea City.

23 November 2006

Northern Ireland international Grant McCann joined Barnsley in a club record deal worth £100,000.

24 November 2001

Cheltenham were beaten 3–0 in their first Football League meeting with Oxford United, with key midfielder Mark Yates missing due to suspension.

24 November 2009

John Schofield picked up his only win as Cheltenham Town's caretaker manager, 5–1 against Barnet. It was Cheltenham's first home win since the opening day of the season and ended a run of 12 games without a victory. Winger Ben Marshall, on loan from Stoke City, scored twice, with Justin Richards and Andy Gallinagh also finding the net along with an own goal from Ismail Yakubu.

25 November 1933

Cheltenham beat Barnet 5–1 in the FA Cup first round with 2 goals each from Horace Payne and George Knight, with another from Harold Yarwood. The match was seen by 6,000 people. It was the Robins' first appearance in the competition proper.

25 November 1950

A Cheltenham side including Ron Coltman and Roy Shiner went down 3–1 at Reading's Elm Pack in the FA Cup first round. Their goal was scored by Vernon Crowe.

25 November 2008

Cheltenham stunned Leeds United with a 1–0 win at Whaddon Road, thanks to Steven Gillespie's 86th minute goal – it gave Keith Downing his first victory as Robins manager. The game was watched by 7,043 fans. Cheltenham: Higgs, Gill, Caines, Duff, Wright, Vincent (Lindegaard) Bird, Sinclair, Spencer, Connor (Madjo), Gillespie. Subs not used: Brown, Gallinagh, D'Agostino.

26 November 1938

Cheltenham drew 1–1 with Cardiff City at home in the FA Cup first round, their goal scored by Steve Prior. They lost the replay 1–0.

26 November 2011

Mark Yates' Cheltenham won 3–1 at Oxford United, their seventh straight win on the road. The goals came from Sido Jombati, who notched his first Football League goal, Kaid Mohamed and Jimmy Spencer. Oxford had Liam Davis sent off ten minutes into the second half.

27 November 1937

Cheltenham lost 3–0 at Watford in an FA Cup first-round replay.

27 November 1976

Goals from John Davies and Wayne Thomas earned Cheltenham a 2–0 FA Trophy second qualifying round win over Dudley Town. Cheltenham: Miles, Murphy, Dangerfield, Foster, Dean, Paterson, Thomas, Gardner, Davies, Hehir, Reid.

27 November 1996

Cheltenham lost their FA Cup first-round tie against Peterborough United 3–1 after extra time. Jimmy Smith scored their consolation goal from the penalty spot after Bob Bloomer had been tripped. Highlights of the match were shown on the BBC's *Sportsnight*.

27 November 1999

Lee Howells scored his first Football League goal in Cheltenham Town's 2–0 home win over Leyton Orient. Neil Howarth was the other scorer.

28 November 2010

Cheltenham were beaten 3–0 by Southampton at the St Mary's Stadium in the second round of the FA Cup.

28 November 1998

Cheltenham beat Rushden & Diamonds 1–0 in a top-of-the-table Conference clash at Whaddon Road in front of 4,051 fans. Keith Knight scored the only goal of the game, with Steve Book saving a penalty. It was Michael Duff's 100th Robins start.

28 November 2005

Cheltenham thrashed Conference club Woking 5–1 during extra time in the LDV Vans Trophy at Kingfield Stadium at the second attempt, after the first match was abandoned due to heavy fog. The goals came from Steven Gillespie (2), Craig Armstrong, Brian Wilson and Jamie Victory.

29 November 1947

Bishop's Cleeve-bred Peter Goring became the first Cheltenham player to score a hat-trick in the FA Cup proper for Cheltenham Town, in a 5–0 win over Street. It was the Robins' only win in the FA Cup proper between the 1933 defeat of Carlisle United and the 2–1 victory over St Albans in 1991.

29 November 1980

Cheltenham were defeated 4–2 at home by a strong Bedford Town side in the Southern League Midland Division. A crowd of only 295 were present at Whaddon Road to see goals either side of half-time from Norman Pemberton and Clive Boxall. Cheltenham: Latchford, Buckland, Dyer, Ollis, Boxall, Kavanagh, MacKenzie, Tester, Green, Pemberton, Shatford.

30 November 1936

Cheltenham drew 0–0 with Brighton at the Goldstone Ground in the FA Cup first round. They lost the replay 6–0.

30 November 1974

Dave Lewis scored a hat-trick at Bath City as Cheltenham hit back from 3–1 down to win 4–2 in the FA Trophy third qualifying round.

30 November 1991

Lee Howells made his Cheltenham Town debut at Wycombe Wanderers. Wayne Matthews made his first appearance in the same match.

DECEMBER

1 December 1984

Cheltenham suffered their fourth successive league defeat as Willenhall Town beat them 1–0 at Noose Lane in the Southern League Premier Division. Cheltenham: Martyn, Murphy, Scarrott, Collicutt, Cornes, Goff, Hughes, Baverstock, Boyland, Wright, Burford.

1 December 1990

Cheltenham lost 3–0 to Altrincham, piling the pressure on manager John Murphy.

2 December 2000

Cheltenham edged a seven-goal thriller against Barnet, with Hugh McAuley and Julian Alsop both scoring twice in the 4–3 success. Cheltenham: Book, Griffin, Freeman, Banks, McCann, Duff, Yates, Howells, McAuley, Alsop, Grayson (White). Subs not used: Bloomer, Milton, Devaney, Higgs.

2 December 2012

Cheltenham Town were drawn at home to Everton in the third round of the FA Cup, but they still had to edge out old rivals Hereford United in the second round to earn a mouth-watering tie against David Moyes' team.

3 December 1977

Cheltenham beat Bath City 7–1 in the FA Trophy third qualifying round, with Dave Lewis firing off 4 goals. There were also 2 own goals and one from striker John Davies, with 1,047 there to see it.

3 December 2012

Cheltenham drew 1–1 with Hereford United in their FA Cup second-round tie at Whaddon Road in front of the live ESPN cameras.

3 December 1990

John Murphy took charge of Cheltenham for the final time, his second spell in charge lasting just one month. It was a 2–0 defeat by Kidderminster Harriers.

4 December 1990

John Murphy resigned after less than one month in charge of Cheltenham for a second time.

4 December 1995

Cheltenham Town launched a new Youth Training Scheme under boss Chris Robinson.

4 December 1999

Cheltenham drew 0–0 at Rochdale, with Michael Duff making his 150th start and Jamie Victory chalking up his 200th. Steve Book saved a penalty from Tony Ellis after Jason Brissett inexplicably picked up the ball in the area, thinking he had heard the whistle blow. It was Book's second successive spot-kick save.

5 December 1992

Cheltenham Town drew 1–1 at home to AFC Bournemouth in the second round of the FA Cup, with youth trainee Christer Warren netting a memorable leveller in the 83rd minute. It was Cheltenham's first home match against Football League opposition since 1968. Warren had been subjected to jeers and chants of derision by the Whaddon Road crowd earlier in the season, prompting boss Lindsay Parsons to make a public plea to leave him alone. He answered his critics, having replaced Andy Tucker in the 70th minute. His goal, volleyed in with his left foot, was his first at senior level. Ex-Robins striker Peter Shearer had already given Tony Pulis' Bournemouth a 12th-minute lead. Cheltenham: Nicholls, Howells, Willetts, Brown, Vircavs, Tucker (Warren), Lovell, N. Smith, J. Smith, Purdie, Bloomer. Sub not used: Wring.

5 December 1995

Cheltenham beat Gloucester City 4–0 at home in the Dr Marten's Cup second round thanks to goals from Paul Chenoweth, Darren Wright and Jimmy Smith (2).

6 December 1975

Cheltenham won 3–2 at Bromsgrove Rovers with goals from John Davies, Dave Lewis and Colin Hall.

7 December 1999

Cheltenham took part in their first ever Auto Windscreens Shield (Football League Trophy) tie, winning 1–0 at Southend United thanks to Russell Milton's goal.

8 December 2001

Cheltenham beat non-league Hinckley United 2–0 in the second round of the FA Cup, with Julian Alsop and Tony Naylor scoring for the Robins.

9 December 1933

Cheltenham Town earned a famous victory over Football League opposition in the FA Cup, something they would have to wait more than sixty years to achieve again. Cheltenham trailed at the break in front of a crowd of 7,437 at Brunton Park, with Slinger putting the Cumbrians ahead. But Cheltenham improved in the second half and Reg Smith scored an equalising goal. Blake rattled the crossbar for Carlisle and Davis made a super save to deny McBain. Carlisle had Kennedy sent off and Bradley's own goal was enough to take Cheltenham through. In the streets, supporters gathered eagerly, awaiting the result. News of the victory was greeted by exultant shouts of 'Bravo, Cheltenham!' The gate money from the match was £371 19*s* 9*d*. Cheltenham: Davis, Jones, Harris, Lang, Blackburn, Goodger, Payne, Smith, Yarwood, Evans, Hill.

9 December 1994

Cheltenham drew 0–0 at Solihull Borough in the Beazer Homes Premier League in front of a crowd of 312.

10 December 2011

Cheltenham turned on the style to beat promotion rivals Southend United 3–0 at the Abbey Business Stadium with goals from Jimmy Spencer, Russ Penn and Marlon Pack. The match was watched by 4,304 fans.

11 December 2009

Martin Allen's departure from Cheltenham Town was confirmed after a period of gardening leave.

12 December 1983

John Dyer, Player of the Year in 1981/82, left Cheltenham Town.

12 December 1989

Chris Burns scored five times in a 6–0 Midland Floodlit Cup win over Alvechurch at Whaddon Road. The other goal came from Paul Sanderson.

13 December 1947

Cheltenham lost 4–2 to Hull City in the FA Cup second round at Boothferry Park. A special train left Lansdown Station at 5.30 a.m., taking fans to the match.

13 December 1986

Brian Hughes missed the Conference match at Northwich due to a stomach upset. It was the only game he missed of the 169 Cheltenham played after he joined. In that time he scored 51 goals, 20 of which were penalties.

13 December 2005

Cheltenham beat Oxford 2–1 in an FA Cup second-round replay with goals from Kayode Odejayi and Brian Wilson.

14 December 1991

Andy Horlick, son of Gerald, went on for his debut as a substitute at Altrincham. Paul Masefield also made his debut, a twenty-year-old released by Birmingham City.

15 December 2001

Cheltenham won 3–1 at York City with 2 goals from Tony Naylor and one from Julian Alsop.

16 December 1989

Cheltenham lost 1–0 at home to Darlington in a top-of-the-table Conference clash in front of 2,662 fans, the club's then highest gate at that level. They went into the match unbeaten in six games and could have gone level with the leaders with a win, but Paul Emson's goal was enough to earn the Quakers all 3 points and Cheltenham's title push faded quickly.

16 December 1992

Cheltenham lost their FA Cup second-round replay 3–0 at AFC Bournemouth, with Denny Mundee, Brian McGorry, and Morgan scoring for the Cherries. More than 1,000 fans from Cheltenham made the trip, making as much, if not more, noise than the Bournemouth crowd. Jimmy Smith shot over with Cheltenham's best chance after being set up by Matt Lovell.

16 December 1997

Cheltenham won an FA Cup second-round replay 2–0 in freezing conditions at Boreham Wood, with goals from Bob Bloomer and Jimmy Smith, setting up a third-round home tie against Reading.

17 December 1988

Cheltenham won a seven-goal thriller against Enfield 4–3 thanks to goals from Nick Jordan, Steve Brooks, Micky Tanner and Steve Crouch.

18 December 1937

Cheltenham won 6–3 for the second match running, beating Tunbridge Wells Rangers away.

18 December 1976

Cheltenham thrashed Worcester City 6–0 in the FA Trophy before a crowd of 811. Six different players scored: Terry Paterson, John Davies, Kieron Hehir, Chris Gardner, Wayne Thomas and Colin Hall. Worcester lost just one league game all season as they won the Southern League Division One (North) championship.

18 December 1983

Alan Wood was sacked and John Murphy was appointed player-manager.

18 December 1990

A crowd of just 594 watched Cheltenham beat Slough Town 2–0 through goals from Steve Brooks and Kim Casey.

18 December 1993

Cheltenham won 1–0 at home to Nuneaton, their sixth straight win and best run since 1982/83. They went on to beat Moor Green before slipping up against Trowbridge Town. Steve Jones scored the decisive goal.

19 December 1997

Cheltenham won a Friday night festive fixture 2–1 at Stevenage Borough, thanks to goals from Jimmy Smith and Dale Watkins. The match is best remembered for a free-kick routine which Steve Cotterill noticed Real Madrid using in a televised match. It involved a feigned mix-up before Watkins turned and smashed in the ball with the Stevenage defence's guard down.

19 December 1998

Cheltenham beat Stevenage 3–0 at home, with Jason Eaton scoring twice and Dale Watkins netting the other goal.

20 December 1947

Cheltenham beat Hereford United 3–2 at Whaddon Road with goals from Jack Harmer, Vernon Crowe and Peter Goring, in front of a crowd of 3,000.

21 December 1963

Cheltenham Town drew 1–1 with Poole Town away thanks to a goal from Allan Palmer.

22 December 2009

Mark Yates was appointed Cheltenham Town's manager, having left Kidderminster Harriers along with assistant Neil Howarth to take charge of the club they both played for together.

23 December 1995

Jimmy Smith scored his 100th Cheltenham Town goal in a 4–1 defeat at Hastings Town.

24 December 1938

Cheltenham beat Newport County Reserves 4–1, with a goal from Billy Ray, two from Steve Prior and an own goal from Lawrence.

24 December 1979

Alan Grundy was appointed manager of Cheltenham Town. His assistant was Graham Allner, who would return to the club as a coach for Steve Cotterill before succeeding him as boss in 2002. Grundy remained boss until 1982.

25 December 1931

The first ever match was played at Whaddon Road, between Cheltenham Town and Tewkesbury Town in the Northern Senior League. Cheltenham won 4–1 with goals from 'Twister' Hazard, Reg Smith and Roy Hill. Cheltenham had moved from Carter's Field in Prestbury Road. The opening was conducted by the Mayor of Tewkesbury. The first goal was scored by Hazard from Hill's corner.

26 December 1966

Cheltenham won 4–2 at Hereford United, with goals from Adrian Thorne, Joe Gadston, Gerald Horlick and Dave Hudd witnessed by 4,463 people.

26 December 1973

Roger Griffiths' goal was enough to sink Gloucester City 1–0 at Horton Road as Cheltenham celebrated a Boxing Day victory.

26 December 1974

Cheltenham enjoyed a 3–1 home win over Gloucester, with goals from Dave Lewis, Dave Dangerfield and an own goal in front of a crowd of 1,548.

26 December 1975

Roger Thorndale made his 702nd and final appearance for Cheltenham Town at Worcester City – a club record unlikely to be broken. He also scored 24 goals. The Robins lost the match 2–1, with Dave Lewis on target.

26 December 1984

Cheltenham beat Gloucester City 4–0 on their way to the Southern League title, with goals from Mark Boyland, Nick Jordan, Steve Cotterill and an own goal from Wayne Stokes. Gloucester were relegated to the Southern League Midland Division that season.

26 December 1988

Cheltenham saw off Newport County 3–2 in front of a crowd of 2,288 with goals from Micky Tanner, Ian Walsh and Nicky Jordan. Micky Nuttell was in the Welsh team's line-up. Newport folded mid-season.

26 December 1994

A crowd of 3,018 gathered at Meadow Park to see Cheltenham beat Gloucester 2–1 with goals from Jason Eaton and Christer Warren. Cheltenham and Gloucester had played each other fifty-seven times in the previous forty-seven years and Cheltenham claimed their thirty-third win – Gloucester had won only nine. Cheltenham: Cutler, Jones, Bloomer, Banks, N. Smith, Cooper, Wring, Warren, J. Smith, Boyle, Eaton. Subs not used: Mortimore, Howells, Cook.

26 December 2000

Steve Book made his 200th start for Cheltenham in a 1–1 home draw against Shrewsbury Town.

26 December 2009

Mark Yates took charge of his first match as Robins boss, resulting in a 1–0 home defeat by Bournemouth.

27 December 1965

Cheltenham enjoyed a 4–0 home win in front of 2,815 spectators over Hereford United, with goals from Gerald Horlick (2), Graham Green and Dave Hudd.

27 December 1993

Cheltenham lost 1–0 at home to Trowbridge Town, with Keith Knight scoring the winner in the 84th minute. It ended a run of seven straight wins. Cheltenham: Heeps, Cooper, S. Jones, Tucker, N. Smith, Brown, Howells, Owen (Wring), J. Smith, Eaton (Mortimore).

28 December 1934

Cheltenham beat Redditch 6–1 at home in front of a crowd of 2,200 with the goals coming from James Currier (2), Vollans, Thomas and Hazard (2). Currier scored 8 goals in 4 games.

28 December 1974

John Davies joined Cheltenham from Gloucester City and scored on his debut in a 1–0 win at Wellingborough Dog & Duck ground in front of 203 fans.

28 December 1987

Brett Angell scored both goals in a 2–1 home win over Weymouth. Cheltenham: Churchward, Baverstock, Willetts, Crowley, Vircavs, Jordan, Townsend, Hughes, Angell, Abbley, Buckland.

28 December 1992

Cheltenham thrashed Gloucester City 4–0, with goals from Jimmy Smith (2), Kevin Willetts and Jason Eaton.

28 December 1998

Dale Watkins scored the only goal of the game as Cheltenham beat Kidderminster Harriers and Steve Books made a breathtaking save from Mark Yates, who joined Cheltenham later in the season.

28 December 1999

Mark Yates scored his first goal for Cheltenham in a 2–1 win at York City.

28 December 2008

Cheltenham lost 6–3 at home to Peterborough United, with goals from Ashley Vincent, Elvis Hammond and Lloyd Owusu. It was Hammond's first goal for the Robins. Cheltenham: Brown, Gallinagh (Owusu), Wright, Kenton, Ridley, Low, Russell, Westlake, Hammond (Hayes), Hayles, Vincent. Subs not used: Connor, Lindegaard, Puddy.

28 December 2009

Mark Yates oversaw his first win as Robins boss 2–0 at Dagenham & Redbridge.

28 December 2010

Cheltenham beat Bradford City 4–0 at Whaddon Road.

29 December 1979

Cheltenham were defeated 2–1 at home by Minehead in the Southern League Midland Division. A crowd of 397 were present at Whaddon Road and Dave Lewis scored the Cheltenham goal in the 66th minute. The late Bobby Stokes, who scored for Southampton in the 1976 FA Cup final, was in the Cheltenham team. Cheltenham: N. Berry, Humphries, Edwards, Davies, Hams, Dangerfield, Higgins, Stokes, Lewis, Reed, Hardcastle.

30 December 1933

Cheltenham beat Birmingham Trams 8–1 with goals from Jesse Goodger, Horace Payne, Harold Yarwood (2), Roy Hill and Albert Evans.

30 December 1989

Cheltenham beat Wycombe Wanderers 4–0 with Mark Buckland scoring a hat-trick and Steve Mardenborough netting the other.

31 December 1938

Cheltenham lost 8–1 to Arsenal Reserves, with Harry Butt the scorer of their goal.

31 December 1983

Cheltenham were defeated by Corby Town 1–0 at their old Occupation Road ground. Recently appointed boss John Murphy continued in a playing role and the crowd numbered just 183.

31 December 1994

Lee Howells scored 2 late goals to rescue a point for Cheltenham Town at Worcester City's St George's Lane.

31 December 2005

Steven Gillespie's goal earned Cheltenham their third consecutive 1–0 win, at home to Shrewsbury Town.